100

*F*AVORITE

*G*ARDEN

WILDFLOWERS

100 FAVORITE GARDEN WILDFLOWERS

TERI DUNN

MetroBooks

DEDICATION

With thanks to my many wildflower friends and colleagues over the years: Bill Brumback, Robert Buchsbaum, Gordon DeWolf, Neil "The Prairie Dog" Diboll, Alton Harvill, Kim Hawks, Gordon Hayward, Everett Holt King, Erik Kiviat, Bill Maple, Bill McDorman and Barbi Reed, Carol Bishop Miller, John Mitchell and Ann Hecker, Gordon Morrison, the late Jerry Sedenko, Andrea Sessions and Marty Zenni, Bruce Sorrie, Kathryn Venezia, and everyone at the Friday night NEBC meetings. This book is dedicated with love to Joe, Frank, Leenie, Kathy, Julie, and Jim.

MetroBooks

An Imprint of Friedman/Fairfax Publishers

©1999 by Michael Friedman Publishing Group, Inc.

Library of Congress Cataloging-in-Publication Data available upon request.

ISBN 1-56799-641-8

Editor: Susan Lauzau
Art Director: Jeff Batzli
Layout Designer: Meredith Miller
Photography Editor: Amy Talluto
Production Manager: Niall Brennan

Color separations by Ocean Graphic International Company Ltd
Printed in Singapore by KHL Printing Co Pte Ltd.

1 3 5 7 9 10 8 6 4 2

For bulk purchases and special sales, please contact:
Friedman/Fairfax Publishers
Attention: Sales Department
15 West 26th Street
New York, NY 10010
212/685-6610 FAX 212/685-1307

Visit our website:
http://www.metrobooks.com

Photography credits:

Front jacket photography: ©Dency Kane (inset); ©Jerry Pavia (background)
Back jacket photography: ©Charles Mann

©Derek Fell: pp. 2, 23, 35, 51, 56, 68, 70, 72, 93, 97, 98, 100, 108, 115, 117

©Steve Hamilton: p. 49

©Jessie M. Harris: p. 57

©Dency Kane: pp. 17, 22, 27, 34, 43, 45, 46, 48, 54, 58, 59, 60, 62, 67, 91, 92, 105, 109, 110, 111

©Charles Mann: pp. 9, 29, 47, 53, 64, 84

©Jerry Pavia: pp. 7, 12, 15, 16, 18, 21, 24, 25, 26, 28, 30, 31, 32, 36, 37, 38, 39, 41, 44, 50, 52, 55, 61, 63, 66, 69, 71, 73, 75, 78, 79, 80, 81, 83, 85, 88, 89, 94, 95, 103, 104, 106, 114, 116

©Joanne Pavia: pp. 10, 11, 13, 14, 40, 42, 74, 77, 82, 96, 101, 102, 113

©Louiseann and Walter Pietrowicz: pp. 19, 76

Visuals Unlimited: ©Ross Frid: p. 20; ©Joe McDonald: p. 33; ©Gary W. Carter: p. 65; ©Michael T. Stubben: p. 86; ©Jon Bertsch: p. 87; ©A. Gurmankin: p. 90; ©Ray Dove: p. 99; ©George Loun: p. 107; ©R. Knolan Benfield, Jr.: p. 112

CONTENTS

Introduction

If you enjoy taking walks or hikes in the woods or mountains, you've probably seen lots of different wildflowers, and likely have thought to yourself, "Oh, I wish I could grow that in my yard." Perhaps you've given in to impulse and dug up a few, wrapped them in a piece of tissue or a plastic bag, and transported them home. Even if you got them into the ground right away, however, chances are they died.

This experience does not mean that you cannot grow wildflowers in your garden. It just shows that transplanting from the wild is tricky. Plants growing in the wild are adapted to wild conditions. Their roots wend their way around natural obstacles, such as other roots, rocks, and fallen trees, and even if you succeed in the difficult task of extracting most or all of a root system without damaging it, a mature plant separated from its natural soil is probably doomed. If the soil in your garden is not similar, the plant may perish on those grounds alone. In the case of pink lady's slipper, for example, transplanting is an even greater risk, because the roots of these wild orchids depend on a delicate relationship with naturally occurring soil fungi. Also, few plants, even the most durable-looking wildflowers, appreciate being moved when they are in bloom.

To get a spectacular wildflower display at home, begin with nursery-raised plants. When purchased from reputable sources, they are young, well-rooted plants (raised from seeds, cuttings, or divisions), which transplant best. And because they have not been subjected to the stress of life in the woods or fields, their foliage is healthy and uniform. Before long, they will bring all the color and beauty to your garden that you dreamed of.

You will be delighted to discover that wildflowers tend to be tougher than other garden plants. If they hail from your area, they are already adapted to local climate and soils, as well as area pests and diseases. If they are not, well, you may still be able to grow them, as long as you can meet their needs. Prairie plants, for instance, are not just for residents of the Midwest; those in the East or West may well succeed with them, too.

Note that some wildflowers are short-lived, while others will be with you forever. Some will stay put, some will spread or self-sow. So read carefully the descriptions here, and do further research in more specialized books if you have lingering questions.

Shopping for Wildflowers

As with any other new garden acquisition, you need to be a wise consumer. Will the wildflower that has captured your fancy grow in the soil or light or moisture conditions found in your yard? The ones described in the following pages were selected because they are good garden subjects; if your wildflower is not here, it may be too difficult to domesticate.

Next, be savvy about your source: you don't want to dig up plants in the wild, or buy ones that someone else has plundered. In years past, the biggest offenders were wholesale suppliers to retail nurseries, and gardeners sometimes ended up with plants that died soon after coming home. Ethical nurseries and concerned botanists spread the word to gardeners and put pressure on the culprits. These days, the chances of finding wild-collected wildflowers for sale are diminished. Be suspicious, though, if the plants look irregular or are not well rooted in their pots, or if your source cannot say whether they were nursery-propagated ("nursery grown" is not necessarily the same thing). Another clue is price. Nursery-propagated trout lilies will never sell ten for five dollars.

Fortunately, you can get garden-ready wildflowers from well-stocked nurseries and from a number of mail-order nurseries that specialize in native plants (these are listed in

the Sources section at the back of this book). If you shop locally, examine your choices carefully to make sure they look healthy and are well rooted. If you shop by mail, open the box immediately upon arrival, remove the packing material, and examine your purchases for the same qualities. Remember, in either case, that a good, strong root system is more important than a lot of green foliage and flowers on top—those will come once your wildflowers are in the ground.

What about growing wildflowers from seed? Certain ones are so quick and easy that it seems silly to buy them as potted plants—for example, columbines and California poppy. On the other hand, there are many wildflowers that are slow or difficult to sprout, such as trilliums and bloodroot. In these cases, you are better off letting the nursery do the work for you and paying the extra charge for their time and expertise. Of course, as you gain experience and confidence, you may become interested in learning all the special germinating techniques and doing this work yourself; there are good books to guide you on this journey (see the list of Further Reading section at the end of this book).

One final note: think twice before you buy a "wildflower meadow in a can." These mixes are frequently designed for quick color the first year and seldom live up to their promise in ensuing years. Others are poorly balanced, meaning that in time more vigorous plants overwhelm their fellows. Also, read the label! Many of these mixes contain aggressive grasses as filler. This does not mean you should never buy a mix. Just shop with care, looking for one that is adapted to your region or conditions (and one that contains no grass seed).

PLANTING WILDFLOWERS

Whether native or slightly out of its range, a wildflower brought into the garden appreciates a little soil preparation. If grass or weeds have been growing in the chosen spot, dig them out. Young wildflowers are no different from other young plants in that they need a chance to get started without being crowded out. Adding organic matter to the soil is often a good idea. It will increase the moisture-holding capacity of dry or sandy soil and lighten compacted or clay-laden soil.

Autumn is a good time to plant wildflowers in all but the harshest climates. The soaking rains this time of year help plant root systems get established. Wildflowers planted in the spring should be sheltered from hot sun and stiff breezes, and watered often until they are well established. In either case, mulching lightly around the base of the plant is generally wise—the mulch will help conserve water, moderate soil-temperature fluctuations, and prevent frost-heaving over the winter.

Remember as you plant to take into account your wildflower's mature size. This is listed at the top of each page (of course, actual dimensions in your garden may vary). Some wildflowers get quite large and sprawling, and while you can cut them back if need be, it is easier to site and space them well at the outset. If you are aiming for a

groundcovering effect, or a carpet of color, closer spacing is, of course, the way to go. For wildflowers that self-sow or spread by creeping roots, if you have the patience, you may simply plant a few at wide intervals and let them fill in over the years.

WILDFLOWER GARDEN DESIGN

There are whole books devoted to this fascinating topic, but you should be aware of a few issues at the outset. First, bear in mind that all the flowers we now cherish in our gardens have their origins in the wild. The ones that have been most successfully domesticated are predictable in performance and uniform in appearance. This cannot always be said of wildflowers. So you need to expect variability—not just in your garden's particular conditions, but within a plant grouping, and even in individual plants. What this means in terms of garden design is a looser, informal look. If that appeals to you, you will be happy with your wildflowers.

This does not mean you have to be bound to a casual-looking garden. Many wildflowers combine very well with the most domesticated flowers—threadleaf coreopsis is wonderful among the highly mannered lavenders, for instance; Virginia bluebells are enchanting among traditional spring bulbs like daffodils; and blazing star is a good companion for some roses. Do what you like. If you need ideas, study garden-design books, browse magazine articles, or visit a botanical garden that displays wildflowers.

Another thing you should be aware of is that some wildflowers can grow aggressively. Each autumn, unless you intervene and deadhead beforehand, they will shed their seeds, and the following spring you will have many more than you started with, sometimes in unexpected nooks and crannies. Or your wildflowers may spread by underground runners, poking up volunteers nearby as well as many feet away. Plan for this tendency and you will end up pleased with great swaths of foliage and carpets of color, or with plants you enjoy digging up and giving away or selling. The alternative is to fight a constant battle, which takes the joy out of gardening.

The unpredictable nature of wildflowers also means that your garden will look different from one year to the next. One summer the bachelor's buttons or California poppies, annuals that often self-sow, will be spectacular; the next year they may not return in glory, but the biennial mulleins and evening primroses will have come into their own.

CARING FOR WILDFLOWERS

Don't assume that just because it's a wild species a wildflower doesn't need any care. Nurture the seedlings just as you would with any prized garden plants. Water them when they need it. And keep their sites well weeded—just a month or two of neglect, and they may get swallowed up by a jungle of aggressive grasses and invasive weeds. Generally, wildflowers do not need to be fertilized, however. Fertilizer tends to cause lush vegetative growth at the expense of flowers.

As the years go by, your wildflowers will require less and less care. The effort you put into their debut in your garden will be repaid in lovely flowering plants, perhaps now spread out in drifts like you originally imagined. If you're like me, you'll be peering over them carefully to monitor their progress. You may be gratified to notice details about your garden-grown wildflowers that you never noticed in the woods or mountain meadows, where you were just passing through.

Achillea millefolium

Yarrow

BLOOM TIME: summer

HEIGHT/WIDTH: $1'-3' \times 1'$ (30–90cm $\times$ 30cm)

LIGHT: full sun

ZONES: 4–8

Yarrow

Too often maligned as a weed, common yarrow has in recent times been rediscovered by horticulturists who admired its good qualities and made selections that broadened the color choices. The plant is a trooper, blooming all summer, even in hot and dry ones, and weathering cold winters. If yarrow is given the full sun and well-drained soil that it favors, it becomes invasive and/or self-sows in unexpected places unless you keep after it—or unless you make sure to plant it in a spot where you are happy to see it naturalize.

The species has flat white flower heads and aromatic, finely dissected gray-green leaves, making it an agreeable companion to other herbs or a filler among colorful sun-loving perennials and annuals. You can grow a colorful cultivar, such as the vibrant cherry red 'Cerise Queen', the deep pink 'Rosea', or a host of other possibilities, including the obvious—sowing a mix (available from many seed companies). All of these are great for bouquets, fresh or dried, thanks to their erect stems and ability to hold their color well past harvest.

Allium cernuum

Nodding onion

BLOOM TIME: summer

HEIGHT/WIDTH: 8"–2' × 6" (20–60cm × 15cm)

LIGHT: full sun

ZONES: 4–8

Nodding onion

In recent years, species onions have come into vogue as ornamental plants. These are related to the ones you grow in the vegetable garden, but some are smaller and less pungent, and have downright pretty, lilylike flowers. And they are simple to grow, particularly when you are not as concerned about developing perfect roots. A sunny setting in decent soil is all they ask. One of the best is a native North American plant called nodding onion.

As the name says, it has flower heads that bend over modestly at the top. They are a loose mop of soft pink, attractive as solo performers here and there in a rock garden but also nice for mingling with pastel perennials or old-fashioned roses. A few variations are to be found at specialty nurseries and bulb suppliers, among them the soft white _A. cernuum_ 'Album'.

Just one caveat: like its kin, this onion sheds its seeds liberally each autumn, leading to great numbers of volunteers the following spring. To discourage such behavior, simply remove (deadhead) the spent blossoms before they go to seed.

Amsonia tabernaemontana

Bluestar

BLOOM TIME: spring–early summer

HEIGHT/WIDTH: $2'$–$3' \times 2'$–$3'$ (60–90cm $\times$ 60–90cm)

LIGHT: full sun–partial shade

ZONES: 3–9

Bluestar

It's hard to find true-blue flowers, in the wild or in fancy garden settings (rose breeders have still had no luck producing a blue rose, for instance). But here is the genuine article. Bluestar's blossoms are about a half-inch across and star-shaped, and appear in domed clusters at the tops of the stems. The tidy foliage, between 3 inches (7cm) and 6 inches (15cm) long, is narrow and willowy and encircles the stems.

Despite these seemingly delicate qualities, the plant is strong and tough, standing erect and thriving in moderately fertile soil. (It can be grown in some shade and in richer soil but will become leggy and need to be trimmed back occasionally to keep growth dense.) Bluestar is also usually free of disease and pest problems. Autumn foliage is a real plus: instead of fading away, the leaves turn a vibrant shade of gold that looks wonderful in the company of autumn bloomers like asters and mums.

Bluestar is probably best grown in groups or sweeps, so its fine texture won't be lost and the wonderful shade of blue has a chance to really stand out. It's also a striking companion for orange- or red-flowered deciduous azaleas, which generallybloom at the same time.

Anaphalis margaritacea

Pearly everlasting

BLOOM TIME: late summer

HEIGHT/WIDTH: 1'–3' × 1'–2' (30–90cm × 30–60cm)

LIGHT: full sun

ZONES: 3–8

Pearly everlasting

The name of this sturdy plant is ideal: the white flower heads have a pearly hue (and, one could say of the individual flowers, a pearly shape), and they preserve so well that they are highly esteemed by dried flower arrangers and wreath-makers. If you wish to grow everlastings and want guaranteed success, start here. Note that the foliage is silvery, and the sturdy yet flexible stems are woolly and white, so you can feature the entire plant in your craft projects. Begin harvesting shortly after the flowers appear.

A true drought-buster that can become invasive, pearly everlasting would be a good candidate for a spot that you have otherwise given up on as productive garden space, such as a curb strip or side yard. Its neutral appearance also makes it a nice backdrop or foil for more vivid flowers, especially pink or purple ones.

Note that this is a perennial plant, usually sold as seed (it grows quickly). Male and female flowers appear on separate plants; but if you sow the better part of a packet, you'll have plenty of both, and the differences between the two will strike you as minor.

Anemone pulsatilla
(Pulsatilla vulgaris)

Pasque-flower

BLOOM TIME: spring

HEIGHT/WIDTH: 8"–10" × 6"–9" (20–25cm × 15–23cm)

LIGHT: full sun

ZONES: 3–7

Pasque-flower

Pasque-flower is one of the earliest perennials to bloom, and what a welcome sight it is. Furry buds spring open to display big yet delicate blooms in softest purple, with golden stamens in the center. (A selection called 'Budapest' has pale blue flowers.) The stems are also furry. When the entire plant is backlit by the pale sunlight of early spring, the sight is truly enchanting.

The common name refers to the fact that these blooms often appear right around the Easter and Passover holidays (in fact, "pasque" comes from the Hebrew word "pesakh," which means "a passing over"). When the flowers fade, puffs of similar-hued silky plumes take over and hang on for many weeks. Sometimes, blooming flowers and these graceful plumes are on the same plant at the same time—an intriguing sight. The leaves, by the way, are also attractive; they are reminiscent of small, furry carrot foliage.

In the wild, this plant favors dry soil that drains well, such as banks, roadsides, and ridges, so it is a natural for a dry rock garden, where it will establish itself and carry on for many years. Some gardeners also have had good luck growing it, because of its small stature, at the front of a flower border or along a path.

Anemonella thalictroides

Rue anemone

BLOOM TIME: spring

HEIGHT/WIDTH: 6"–10" × 4"–6" (15–25cm × 10–15cm)

LIGHT: partial shade

ZONES: 5–8

Rue anemone

Many spring wildflowers have a brief show; this one keeps on blooming for up to six weeks. If you have a semishady, somewhat sheltered area and are seeking a delicately beautiful groundcover that you can get a surprising amount of mileage out of, look no further. All rue anemone requires is organically rich soil. It grows from a tuberous root, best planted in autumn when you're doing your bulb plantings.

The flowers are sweet little things, with frail petals and a tiny spray of jaunty stamens. They are usually creamy white, but occasionally soft pink. If you especially like the pink, you might want to seek out the selection 'Schoaf's Double Pink'.

Rue anemone foliage is equally dainty. As the *"thalictroides"* part of the botanical name suggests, it resembles that of meadow rue (*Thalictrum*), just, of course, much smaller and shorter. It precedes the blooms and remains for a while after they pass, but eventually, long about midsummer, the plant goes dormant.

Aquilegia canadensis

Columbine

BLOOM TIME: spring–early summer

HEIGHT/WIDTH: 1'–3' × 1'–2' (30–90cm × 30–60cm)

LIGHT: full sun–partial shade

ZONES: 3–9

Columbine

If you are new to wildflower gardening, and want sure success, grow this charmer. Columbine takes quickly and easily to garden conditions and has unusually pretty flowers, and its handsome, lacy foliage is an asset long after blooming is over.

The nodding, upside-down blossoms make it worth getting down on your hands and knees for a closer look. Generally, the spurred outer petals are red and the fluted inner ones are bright yellow. Golden-tipped stamens hang down like bell clappers. Nectar is located in the spurs, and hummingbirds, with their long tongues, will sometimes visit. Bees cannot reach in that far, but have been observed landing on top and poking a hole in to feed.

If you enjoy this species, wonderful variations await you. Another wild species carried by some seed companies is the state flower of Colorado, *A. caerulea*, with blue and white flowers. And there are many larger-flowered garden hybrids, some solid colors, many bicolors, and some with fluffy "double" forms.

Columbine's only flaw is that its lacy foliage is prone to leaf miners, which weave their trails inside the leaves until little green is left. The flowers keep on blooming, though, seemingly unaffected. Remove all affected foliage, or wait until flowering is over and cut the entire plant down. A fresh flush of new foliage will appear shortly after.

Arctostaphylos uva-ursi

Bearberry, kinnikinick

BLOOM TIME: spring

HEIGHT/WIDTH: 6" × 8"–20" (15cm × 20–51cm)

LIGHT: full sun–partial shade

ZONES: 2–7

'Massachusetts' bearberry

This trailing plant may be one of nature's favorite ground-covers—and, if you have the right conditions in your yard, it could become one of yours. In spring, it sports tiny, nodding pinkish or white bells (if you definitely want pink blooms, plant its near its cousin, *A. nevadensis*). A cultivar, 'Massachusetts', flowers more heavily and has denser, darker foliage than the species. From spring through summer, the neat little glossy green leaves form a dense mat. In autumn, the bright red berries appear and the foliage often acquires a bronze hue. The berries are too mealy to be tasty to people and most birds, so the autumn show—which persists into early winter in milder areas—looks downright Christmassy (though picked sprigs, unfortunately, shrivel and wilt indoors).

Bearberry is related to heaths and heathers and, like those stalwarts, tolerates bitterly cold winters and dry summers. It performs best in sunny spots in acidic soil. Boggy conditions lead to its demise—instead, plant it in well-drained, even sandy, soil. This combination of requirements, plus its tough constitution, means bearberry might be just the plant for an otherwise inhospitable bank or streetside area—over the years, it will carpet an increasingly large area. Bearberry will also do well under the high shade of evergreens, where few other plants grow.

Argemone mexicana

Prickly poppy

BLOOM TIME: spring–autumn

HEIGHT/WIDTH: 1'–3' × 1'–2' (30–90cm × 30–60cm)

LIGHT: full sun

ZONES: 7–9

Prickly poppy

Sure, it's got bristly stems, spiny-edged leaves that remind you of thistles, and prickly seed capsules, but, ah, those gorgeous golden flowers! And they literally cover the plant from spring to first frost—an irresistible performance.

A wild relative of the more familiar garden Oriental poppies, this species has the same sort of flower: large, crinkly petals centered by a fluffy boss of stamens. Prickly poppy is a bit of a novelty because it is yellow through and through (or, sometimes, orange). A near relative is the white-flowered, yellow-centered A. *platyceras*. These plants are not long-lived, alas, but they do self-sow well. They look best in a wild garden, perhaps with some grasses (they'll hold their own in the company of aggressive growers). For a patch of glowing color, sow them with California poppy.

Native to dry grasslands and desert areas, prickly poppies are just as tough and drought-tolerant as you might expect. Once a colony gets established, they are practically no-maintenance. Just remember that good drainage is a must.

Arisaema triphyllum

Jack-in-the-pulpit

BLOOM TIME: spring

HEIGHT/WIDTH: 2'–3' × 1' (60–90cm × 30cm)

LIGHT: partial–full shade

ZONES: 4–8

Jack-in-the-pulpit

Arguably not an especially beautiful wildflower, at least not in the traditional sense, this woodland North American native has an eccentrically elegant look. Each plant grows two stalks; one bears a pair of leaf-topped stems, the other bears the odd-looking flowering structure. A green-and-maroon-striped hood that curves over at the top, the "pulpit" shields "Jack," a slender, dark red-brown and white spadix. The true flowers lurk at the bottom of the spadix and are very tiny. Through it all, the broad leaves, borne in leaflets of three, form a canopy over the show.

In autumn, if the plant is growing in rich, moist soil and prospering, a cluster of oval red berries appears, sheathed in a papery cylinder. They are not edible. Unless you plan to collect one and sow the seed, however, for the good of the plants long-term vigor, you should remove the berries.

Those gardeners with woodland conditions will find Jack-in-the-pulpit easy to grow. Moist soil is essential. The plant is tedious to grow from seed, taking up to four years to reach blooming size. Better to start with a seedling that has already developed its corm (a bulblike root).

You will be intrigued to learn that this plant's Asian relatives are now making it into specialty catalogs. Some have textured or marbled foliage and stems, dramatic colors, and a few have orange autumn berries.

Asarum canadense

Wild ginger

BLOOM TIME: spring

HEIGHT/WIDTH: 4"–12" × 4"–6" (10–30cm × 10–15cm)

LIGHT: shade

ZONES: 5–8

Wild ginger

If your shady garden needs a dense, dependable ground-cover, look no further. The lustrous green, heart-shaped leaves of wild ginger are handsome, and over the years the plant forms broad, thick patches. The leaves look like they should be evergreen, but they are not; however, the plants return with gusto each spring. The only threat to their well-being is slugs, so be on the lookout.

Wild ginger's flowers are not a reason to grow the plant, for they are hidden under the leaf cover at the base; but they are fascinating. They are tiny things, reddish inside, gray-green outside; one botanist aptly likened them to "little brown stone crocks." They last for many weeks, and when they pass, the seeds are carried off by small creatures.

The plant gets its name from its root, which has an appealing, gingerlike scent and flavor. Native Americans used it in cooking and medicinally. It is not related to commercial ginger root.

Asclepias tuberosa

Butterfly weed

BLOOM TIME: summer

HEIGHT/WIDTH: 1'–3' × 1'–2' (30–90cm × 30–60cm)

LIGHT: full sun–partial shade

ZONES: 3–9

Butterfly weed

An orange this vivid is not often seen in gardens. Adventurous garden colorists, though, absolutely should not be without butterfly weed. It will set your summer borders afire. Pair it with the long-blooming golden daylily 'Stella d'Oro' or yellow coreopsis or brilliant purple blooms such as veronica. If you want its glow, but not as the center of attention, grow it with white or blue flowers. Butterfly weed is also excellent in a vase, with erect stems and durable blossoms that last a week or more.

Humans aren't the only ones drawn to this wildflower. Monarch and swallowtail butterflies, bumblebees, and even hummingbirds hover around it. Part of the satisfaction of growing butterfly weed is knowing that your garden welcomes such visitors.

A drought-tolerant plant, butterfly weed develops a thick taproot, so put it where you want it to stay. It survives best on benign neglect; don't coddle it with rich soil, mulch, extra water, or fertilizer. Once it is several years old, you may mow it down after it blooms to inspire a second round of blooms in late summer or early autumn.

Aster nova-angliae

New England aster, Michaelmas daisy

BLOOM TIME: late summer–autumn

HEIGHT/WIDTH: 3'–4' × 2'–3' (90cm–1.2m × 60–90cm)

LIGHT: full sun

ZONES: 4–8

New England aster

Here's a wildflower that had to travel overseas, and back, before Americans would take it seriously as a garden plant. It has many natural virtues, including abundant color for many weeks late in the season, robust growth, and reliable winter-hardiness. The species is a hearty plant covered with clouds of small, light purple daisies. European plant breeders renamed this wildflower Michaelmas daisy (because it blooms around that autumn holiday), and worked with it and some closely related varieties to create a range of fabulous cultivars. Among their triumphs is the popular, large-flowered, electric pink 'Alma Potschke'. A more recent introduction is the mounding, bloom-laden 'Purple Dome'.

As they grow, New England asters form clumps, develop woody stems, and may require staking to support upright growth. The leaves are lance-shaped, and the lower ones tend to drop, leaving the plants bare-kneed (if this bothers you, plant something shorter in front of them).

Balsamorhiza sagittata

Arrowleaf balsamroot

BLOOM TIME: spring

HEIGHT/WIDTH: 1'–3' × 1'–2' (30–90cm × 30–60cm)

LIGHT: full sun

ZONES: 4–7

Arrowleaf balsamroot

If you live in the Mountain West, or have traveled there, perhaps you've admired this bright, daisylike wildflower. It puts on quite a show for many weeks in spring, sporting large, cheerful yellow, 2- to 4-inch (5 to 10cm) flowers that surge above big, arrowhead-shaped leaves.

To grow it in your garden, you need fertile, well-drained soil that is slightly alkaline, like the hillsides from which it comes. If you start from seed, you also need patience; arrowleaf balsamroot takes a few years to reach blooming size. By that time, it will have developed a strong, deep root system that ensures its long-term survival. Just be sure to sow it where you want it to stay, because it is a notoriously poor transplanter.

This is not a plant that needs coddling. Your best bet is to mimic the conditions it enjoys in nature: keep it watered in the spring if rainfall seems sparse, then let it dry out as summer hits its stride.

Baptisia australis

False blue indigo

BLOOM TIME: early summer

HEIGHT/WIDTH: 3'–6' × 3' (90cm–1.8m × 90cm)

LIGHT: full sun–partial shade

ZONES: 3–9

False blue indigo

A picture in blue, this shrubby perennial wildflower has blue-green foliage and 10-inch (25cm) spikes of lavender-blue flowers that stay in bloom for up to a month. It is a member of the pea family, which also includes sweet peas and lupines, and you can easily see the resemblance both in the leaflets and in the classic flower form.

Simple to grow, false blue indigo requires only well-drained soil. As in its wild habitat, it does fine in poor to average soil. Just be sure to place it where you want it to stay, because it forms a deep taproot that makes later transplanting an ordeal. It is disease- and pest-free. False blue indigo is at home in a casual, cottage garden setting, or you could devote a slope or curbside planting to it.

When the flowers fade, they are replaced by brown, pendulous pods that some people enjoy harvesting for dried-flower arrangements or as a rattling toy for a child or cat. But if you cut off the blooms before they go to seed, you can also coax the plant into blooming longer.

Baptisia pendula

White indigo

BLOOM TIME: spring

HEIGHT/WIDTH: 2'–4' × 2'–3' (60cm–1.2m × 60–90cm)

LIGHT: full sun–partial shade

ZONES: 5–9

White indigo

Tall and regal, white indigo is certain to elicit admiration from everyone who visits your garden. It begins as a modest clump of sage green foliage; in late spring, once it is established, expect 3- to 4-foot panicles of soft white, pealike flowers. The stems (and older flower buds) are charcoal gray, making a dramatic contrast with the purity of the flowers. It's quite a sight.

White indigo is also a cinch to grow. Average soil in sun or a bit of shade suits it just fine. Give it extra water and perhaps some mulch the first year or two, and it will form a large, deep root system that will stand it in good stead through future periods of drought. Thereafter, white indigo will take care of itself and bloom more profusely with each passing year.

Because of its stature and somewhat shrubby habit, white indigo is a good choice for the back of a flower border. It is equally at home among roses and cottage garden flowers, and other wildflowers. A natural combination is interplanting it with false blue indigo (*Baptisia australis*).

Belamcanda chinensis

Blackberry lily

BLOOM TIME: midsummer

HEIGHT/WIDTH: 1'–3' × 8"–12" (30–90cm × 20–30cm)

LIGHT: full sun

ZONES: 5–10

Blackberry lily

This unusual, easygoing plant gets its name not from its flower, but from the contents of its autumn pod, which splits open to reveal a seed cluster that looks just like a ripe, succulent blackberry. Unfortunately, it doesn't taste anything like one and in fact is rarely nibbled on by any creature. Some gardeners enjoy harvesting the "berries" to include in wreaths or dried-flower arrangements.

The 2- to 3-inch, star-shaped flower that precedes this interesting seedpod stands out in the garden, bright orange with reddish-purple speckles (some books and catalogs therefore call it the leopard lily). The plant forms clumps and produces long, flat leaves that look like iris foliage (it is actually in the iris, not the lily, family). Like irises, blackberry lily grows from a rhizome that should be planted shallowly and divided every few years to keep the show going.

Blackberry lily asks only for adequate sun and average soil. Those needs met, you can look forward to it providing two seasons of intrigue.

Apparently it came over with early American colonists and eventually escaped the bounds of their gardens. It has jumped back over the garden fence in the past decade or so and is not hard to find in well-stocked garden centers and nursery catalogs.

Boltonia asteroides

Boltonia

BLOOM TIME: late summer–autumn

HEIGHT/WIDTH: 4'–6' × 2'–4' (1.2–1.8m × 60cm–1.2m)

LIGHT: full sun

ZONES: 4–9

'Snowbank' boltonia

An exuberant plant, boltonia has become the darling of gardeners who want weeks of showy color in late summer and autumn. It literally billows with hundreds of small 1-inch (2.5cm) daisies, white with yellow centers, that look perky all day and really light up the garden in the evening hours. They are carried on strong stems on a casual mound of thin, willowy, gray-green foliage. The plant can get quite large, to 6 feet (1.8m) tall, and may require staking to keep it from flopping over. You can also seek out the more modest-size cultivars. The popular 'Snowbank' grows to between 3 and 4 feet (90cm–1.2m). There is also a pink-flowered one of about the same size called 'Pink Beauty'.

An easy plant to grow, boltonia asks only for plenty of sun. If the soil is naturally moist and fertile, the plant will prosper for years with little attention from you. Even in drier soils, it does well, though it may not grow as tall or as lushly. Grow it with other daisylike wildflowers—it looks wonderful among asters, both the species ones and the cultivated varieties. Another idea is interplanting boltonia with goldenrod so that the golden spikes shoot up and around boltonia's more mounding shape.

Callirhoe involucrata

Wine cups

BLOOM TIME: spring–summer

HEIGHT/WIDTH: 8"–12" × 1'–3' (20–30cm × 30–90cm)

LIGHT: full sun

ZONES: 4–8

Wine cups

Among the many plants often recommended for dry, sunny spots in poor to average soil, including boring junipers and overused dusty millers and artemisias, wine cups is rarely mentioned. Perhaps this is because this native of the Midwestern prairies hasn't been sufficiently publicized. Too bad. It's a terrific choice for such trying conditions, bringing stunning color and plenty of it. Once it's established, its deep taproot prohibits transplanting but assures long-term survival, especially during periods of drought or neglect.

Wine cups is aptly named. The 2-inch (5cm), cup-shaped blooms are somewhat variable, but generally a lovely, vivid magenta—zinfandel red, you might say—with a contrasting white center. The sprawling plant generates loads of these in late spring, and continues to pump them out all summer long, stopping only when frost hits. Now your dry bank, curb strip, or front walk can be full of color.

You also can invite this appealing plant into the garden proper, bearing in mind its low, spreading growth habit. It's pretty with lamb's ears (if you're the sort of gardener who always clips off the rosy flower stalks, you may wish to leave them for contrast, both in form and color). Blue flowers with similarly shaped blooms also make nice companions; try it with mounding *Campanula carpatica* or at the feet of blue flax.

Calochortus spp.

Mariposa lily

BLOOM TIME: late spring–early summer

HEIGHT/WIDTH: 1'–2' × 1' (30–60cm × 30cm)

LIGHT: full sun–partial shade

ZONES: 5–9

Mariposa lily

Visitors to the dry mountains and meadows of western North America in late spring never fail to be captivated by these beautiful wildflowers. With their large, goblet-shaped blooms, they superficially resemble poppies, though they are more closely related to tulips. The color of the silky petals varies from one species to the next: *C. clavatus* has yellow flowers with chocolate markings, the flowers of *C. catalinae* are porcelain white–pink, those of *C. nitidis* are creamy white, *C. splendens* is lavender, and the highly variable *C. venustus* may be anywhere from creamy white to dark red, with contrasting blotches and eye. The name "mariposa" means "butterfly" in Spanish, a likeness no one who has seen a patch in full bloom can deny.

Mariposa lilies have erect branching stems and thin grassy leaves. They grow very slowly from seed, eventually forming a small bulb (which, by the way, is edible). They do go dormant in midsummer, and should be allowed to dry out then, as they would in nature. They tend to bloom fabulously one year and then take a year or two off to regroup. They need conditions similar to what they favor in the wild, and, yes, they require patience. But once established, they take care of themselves, and win your heart all over again.

Caltha palustris

Marsh marigold

BLOOM TIME: spring

HEIGHT/WIDTH: 12"–18" × 9"–12" (30–45cm × 23–30cm)

LIGHT: full sun–partial shade

ZONES: 4–10

Marsh marigold

This sunny-flowered buttercup relative is ideal for wet sites. If you grow it in damp garden soil, it tends to have a short but exuberant period of glory each spring. Consider interplanting it among, or providing a backdrop for, bulbs that don't mind similar conditions, like camas or winter aconite.

After the flowers finally go by, if your soil begins to dry out as summer advances, the foliage of marsh marigold gradually dies down and fades from view and the plant goes dormant (not unlike the behavior of your bulbs, come to think of it). If this leaves you with a bare area, be sure to plant marsh marigold in the company of other bog-loving plants that continue the show, like cardinal flower or irises.

Gardeners with water gardens also value this plant. It will wade right into the shallow water near the edge (up to 6 feet [1.8m] deep). Since it makes runners, the plant is best confined to a large pot. After the flowers fade, the succulent, cabbagelike leaves will remain, particularly if you keep after it with fertilizer.

Marsh marigold flowers really are sensational. They are bright, about 2 inches (5cm) across, and carried in clusters. A cultivar, 'Plena', has double flowers.

Camassia spp.

Camas

BLOOM TIME: early summer

HEIGHT/WIDTH: 1'–2' × 8"–12" (30–60cm × 20–30cm)

LIGHT: full sun

ZONES: 3–8

Camas

Like the buffalo, this gorgeous plant used to be plentiful in the great meadows of the West and its decline can be blamed on the encroachment of European settlers. For centuries, Native American tribes, among them the Bannocks and the Nez Perce, valued camas as a food plant (the small onionlike bulb is edible, raw or roasted) and even fought battles to retain their claims. To this day, springtime visitors to central California, Washington, Idaho, and Utah are awestruck when they happen upon remaining drifts in full bloom, which have been likened to lakes of clear blue water.

The good news is that camas is available to gardeners (generally from nurseries in the West but also from specialty bulb catalogs) and easy to grow. As with other bulbs, you should plant them in autumn; camas is also easy to grow from spring-sown seed. In any case, the plants may not bloom their first year, but the flowers are worth waiting for. Tall spikes bear starry, long-lasting blooms. *C. quamash* (*C. esculenta*) is a brilliant blue; *C. cusickii* is light blue; and *C. leichtlinii* ssp. *suksdorfi* 'Alba' is white. They make a fascinating addition to your bulb beds, and are stunning planted among traditional favorites like late-blooming tulips. To emulate their glory in the wild, however, you'll need a damp location in full sun, such as the edge of a pond or a semiwild wet area.

Castilleja spp.

Indian paintbrush

BLOOM TIME: summer

HEIGHT/WIDTH: 1'–2' × 8"–12" (30–60cm × 20–30cm)

LIGHT: full sun

ZONES: 4–9

Indian paintbrush

You may have heard this famous Native American legend. A young boy finds he has a talent for painting but he is continually frustrated in his wish to paint the colors of the sunset, until one night he is directed by a dream-vision to take a canvas up to a nearby hillside. There, he finds fiery red and orange brushes, paints quickly while the light fades, and returns in triumph to his village. In the morning, the hills are abloom with the "paintbrushes" he left behind.

Gardeners often find their pursuit of the Indian paintbrush equally frustrating. The seeds germinate very slowly; they can take at least a year to sprout. Transplants are slow to get established, or don't make it. It turns out that this wildflower's roots have suckers on them that (partially) parasitize the root systems of other plants. Obviously, this characteristic is a tricky situation to re-create at home, though some gardeners have had spectacular success. Your best bet is to start with young plants and tuck them in with companions that they might have had in the wild—other wildflowers, grasses, sages.

The "paintbrush" flowers are technically bracts, and the color varies depending on the species and, sometimes, the setting. *C. linariaefolia* is orange-red; *C. angustifolia* is soft pink; *C. coccinea, C. miniata,* and *C. hispida* are scarlet, and *C. unakaschcensis* is yellow.

Centaurea cyanus

Bachelor's button, cornflower

BLOOM TIME: summer

HEIGHT/WIDTH: 1'–3' × 4"–8" (30–90cm × 10–20cm)

LIGHT: full sun

ZONES: annual, all zones

Bachelor's button

Some gardeners grow this beauty solo, but perhaps its best and most popular use is as an ingredient in a mixed wild-flower planting. (This is why it is often a component in wildflower meadow mixes. For more information on the merits of those, please refer to the Introduction.) It is also a pretty candidate for a cottage garden scheme. Bachelor's button comes in various shades of blue and purple as well as pink and white. The plants bloom eagerly and dependably for the better part of the summer.

It is an easygoing annual plant, not particular about soil or water, though extremes of any kind may do it in. Sow it in full sun, lightly covered (and expect its progeny to self-sow over the ensuing years). If you live in a mild climate, try autumn sowing for a late winter or early spring show; everyone else should sow in spring. It tolerates autumn frosts with admirable perkiness.

The ability of bachelor's button to keep its bright color in the garden holds over in harvest. It is wonderful in casual bouquets, thanks also to its wiry stems. The petals are slow to shatter and are more likely to simply, finally, fade. And as the name suggests, it certainly makes an ideal boutonniere. Wreath-makers and dried-flower arrangers also cherish the blooms because they provide a welcome spot of bright color.

Chasmanthium latifolium

Sea oats

BLOOM TIME: midsummer

HEIGHT/WIDTH: 3'–4' × 2' (1–1.2m × 60cm)

LIGHT: full sun–partial shade

ZONES: 4–9

Sea oats

Ornamental grasses have been all the rage in naturalistic gardens in recent years. While some are admittedly pretty fabulous of leaf or plume, nothing quite matches the shimmering beauty of this native, clump-forming grass.

The bladelike foliage is attractive, particularly early in the season when it has a bluish purple hue. But the "flower" panicles, composed of little spikelets, are the real draw. These come out after summer is well under way, but linger into autumn. As the weather cools, they change from green to maroon to copper before drying out to brown. At any time, they enchant the eye and ear as they rattle and flitter in the breeze. They also make a wonderful contribution to flower arrangements, whether you pick them green or in their autumn splendor. (Do remove them if you don't want the plant to self-sow.)

The fact that this grass tolerates shade well suggests nontraditional uses. It offers a quick screen for the dying-down foliage of spring bulbs, for instance. It would be a novel choice for a solo planting in a container, sited on a deck or porch where no visitor could miss its charms. But perhaps it will get the most attention when you mass it along a fence, walkway, or foundation.

Chelone lyonii

Turtlehead

BLOOM TIME: late summer

HEIGHT/WIDTH: 2'–4' × 1'–2' (60cm–1.2m × 30–60cm)

LIGHT: full sun–partial shade

ZONES: 5–7

Turtlehead

In late summer, there's not much going on in the semishady garden. These lusty pink to reddish purple blooms, then, are a welcome sight. They look somewhat like snapdragons, to which they are distantly related. To say the puffy, lipped flowers resemble the head of a turtle, however, is a bit of a stretch.

Like its namesake, though, turtlehead loves wet places. This plant will thrive in shallow water, a low, muddy spot, or naturally moist soil with the additional insurance of a mulch laid at the plant's base. The exposure is less critical. When it is happy, it will increase quickly. So if you have a good spot, there's no need to start with a lot of plants.

As far as companions go, ferns are always a safe bet. Their dark foliage will set off the colorful flowers to good advantage. If you want to dress up your damp site with additional color, though, consider great blue lobelia or pink obedient plant.

Chrysanthemum leucanthemum

Oxeye daisy

BLOOM TIME: summer

HEIGHT/WIDTH: 1'–3' × 8"–15" (30–90cm × 20–38cm)

LIGHT: full sun

ZONES: 3–9

Oxeye daisy

There are plenty of fancier, cultivated daisies, but this old faithful of field and meadow has enduring appeal. Unlike some other daisies, it carries its blooms on sturdy, unbranched stems—this quality, plus its tendency to bloom profusely, makes it a constant supply of cheery bouquets.

As you might expect, oxeye daisy is no trouble to grow, tolerating all sorts of soils and less than full sun if need be. Its only flaw is its enthusiasm for life; it spreads by rootstock as well as seed. One rhizome can pump out quite a few new little rosettes each season. And one flower head (the center, yellow part, which is where the true, minute flowers reside) can generate upward of three hundred seeds—multiply that by the number of flowers on a single plant, and you see the problem! So be sure to remove fading flowers promptly, and dig under unwanted seedlings. Unless, of course, you want an impromptu meadow in your yard or curb strip.

Occasionally, you will observe a frothy mass along some of the stems. This is the work of the spittlebug, who can suck enough fluid out of the stems to make them bend or become deformed. If this becomes a problem, simply spray it off the stem with the hose or wipe it off with your gloves.

Chrysogonum virginianum

Goldenstar

BLOOM TIME: summer

HEIGHT/WIDTH: 4"–12" × 1'–2' (10–30cm × 30–60cm)

LIGHT: full sun–partial shade

ZONES: 5–9

Goldenstar

For a spot that needs brightening, little goldenstar is unbeatable. A low, spreading (but not aggressive) plant, it has dark green leaves and bears marvelous, glowing yellow, 1½-inch (4cm) daisylike blooms on short stalks. If you grow it in soil that is neither boggy nor dry, it will bloom generously, perhaps even for the whole summer—a claim few other traditional groundcovers can rival.

This wildflower is native to the area from the Appalachians down south to Florida, and will surely thrive in gardens in that part of the country. But goldenstar also does just fine further north, provided you give it a good winter mulch.

Mass plantings, as along a woodland walkway or bordering a line of shrubs, always look great and call attention to the vivacious though small flowers. But you can successfully combine goldenstar with other perennial wildflowers—try it with alumroot, columbine, or Virginia bluebells.

Cimicifuga racemosa

Bugbane

BLOOM TIME: midsummer

HEIGHT/WIDTH: 3'–6' × 3' (1–1.8m × 1m)

LIGHT: full sun–partial shade

ZONES: 3–8

Bugbane

This is a tall, full plant, not for every garden, but spectacular in the right setting. It is best employed in back of shorter plants, where its imposing presence enhances rather than overwhelms; some gardeners like to place it in the middle of an "island bed," where it can be admired from all sides. It is also a bold choice for an area of filtered shade.

Dark green, much-divided foliage creates a bushlike form up to about 3 feet (90m) tall and wide. The creamy white flower plumes, 6 inches (15cm) or more long, rise up an additional 2 or 3 feet (60 to 90cm) above the foliage and are a sight to behold: they are branched, rather than individual spires, so the effect is like candelabras. Bugbane puts on a regal show for several weeks in midsummer, and never needs propping up. Some nurseries don't mention the scent, while others tell you it's "rank," but the truth is that it's not very obtrusive.

Bugbane is long-lived and trouble-free, unfussy about soil and asking only for sufficient moisture. In hot climates, or if you want extra drama from those remarkable flower plumes, grow it in partial shade.

Coreopsis verticillata

Threadleaf coreopsis

BLOOM TIME: summer

HEIGHT/WIDTH: 1'–3' × 2'–3' (30–90cm × 60–90cm)

LIGHT: full sun

ZONES: 5–9

Threadleaf coreopsis

Unlike some other wildflowers, this one looks like a cultivated flower already, without any intervention from plant hybridizers. Its naturally sunny yellow blooms generally cover the plant for most, if not all, of the summer months.

Threadleaf coreopsis brings with it a natural toughness, too. It thrives in a wide range of soils, and adapts easily to drought once established. It does best in full sun.

One unique feature of this particular species—and the reason for its common name—is its thin, needlelike leaves.

The result is an airy plant that weaves its way among taller or more substantial perennials with ease and grace. Because the flowers of threadleaf coreopsis are not large and bold, they flatter their companions while providing dependable color.

If you want a softer hue, look for the cultivar 'Moonbeam', which billows with lovely, pale yellow flowers.

Cornus canadensis

Bunchberry

BLOOM TIME: spring

HEIGHT/WIDTH: 3"–9" (7–23cm)/spreading habit

LIGHT: shade

ZONES: 2–6

Bunchberry

Here is a splendid groundcover for shade. In its native woods, it grows in broad colonies, lighting up the gloom with its large (for its size) white flowers—a sight you may wish to imitate in your garden. It must have humus-rich, moist, well-drained soil to do well, however, so it is happier under deciduous trees or a combination of deciduous and evergreen ones (the ground under a grove of shallow-rooted evergreens is often too dry and infertile). It is also nice at the feet of rhododendrons and azaleas.

Bunchberry flowers look just like those of dogwood trees, which is no surprise, as they are in the same genus. The orange-red berries that follow by autumn are also char-acteristic and, while pulpy to our taste, are beloved by birds. As for the leaves, they grow in a loose whorl around the stem and are a nice, shiny green. In sheltered locations, they may last all winter.

Your best bet is to start with young seedlings; although bunchberry can be grown from seed, this is a tedious process best left to the nursery. Also, older plants tend to be woodier and to resent transplanting. Keep your bunchberry crop well-watered its first season, and add a moisture-retaining mulch. If your plants are happy, they will slowly spread far and wide throughout your shade garden; extras are easily removed.

Cypripedium spp.

Lady's slipper

BLOOM TIME: spring

HEIGHT/WIDTH: 1' × 8" (30cm × 20cm)

LIGHT: partial–full shade

ZONES: 5–8

Lady's slipper

Early spring hikers in woodland areas of the East Coast are frequently treated to the glorious sight of this beautiful wildflower growing under pine or oak trees. Some have succumbed to its charms to the point of digging up a few plants and bringing them home to replant. Alas, like Cinderella at the stroke of midnight, the spell cannot last, and these transplants, which looked so stalwart, soon wilt and die.

If you do the politically and horticulturally correct thing and turn to specialty catalogs that sell nursery-propagated wildflowers, you may again be disappointed. Ethical nurseries don't dig up plants in the wild, knowing the plants won't survive in their customers' gardens. Nor will they buy plants from "freelance poachers," who sometimes offer the plants cheaply and in quantity (and often looking very much worse for wear).

That leaves seed-raised lady's slippers. Those who have tried this report that it takes patience and greenhouse conditions, and that even then the little seedlings sometimes expire when finally transplanted outdoors. Some gardeners have had limited success broadcasting ripe seeds in autumn in a suitable spot (a humusy woodland area).

Otherwise, I'm afraid you'll have to be content with paying an annual visit to your favorite wild patch to admire lady's slippers in situ.

Daucus carota

Queen Anne's lace

BLOOM TIME: summer

HEIGHT/WIDTH: 3'–5' × 1'–3' (1–1.5cm × 30–90cm)

LIGHT: full sun

ZONES: 3–9

Queen Anne's lace

If you think of Queen Anne's lace as a weed, think again. It is a tough, attractive plant that can contribute great beauty to flower beds, herb gardens, and meadow plantings. Because it forms a taproot (as the botanical name suggests, it is related to our cultivated carrot), it is drought-tolerant, making it a good choice for sunny spots in ordinary soil.

Queen Anne's lace is a biennial, which means that it blooms in its second season—and should probably be pulled out after that. If it is surrounded by other plants, it is unlikely to spread much, and you may find yourself in the position of collecting and sowing the seeds to get more plants. The flat-topped, lacy flower heads are fascinating. The outer florets are larger, the inner ones smaller, and in the very center is a lone purple one—botanists have suggested that this arrangement looks like a bullseye to pollinators, which should get their attention! It has also been observed that, in rainy weather, the stem right below the flower head becomes soft enough to nod down, thus shielding its pollen (older flowers that have already lost their pollen don't bend).

As for the charming name, one legend has it that the fourteenth-century English queen, then a young girl, copied the flower form when she learned to tat. A variation says that the queen pricked her finger while making lace, and the tiny purple center floret represents the droplet of her blood.

Dicentra eximia

Wild bleeding heart

BLOOM TIME: spring–summer

HEIGHT/WIDTH: 1'–2' × 1'–3' (30–60cm × 30–90cm)

LIGHT: partial shade

ZONES: 2–9

Wild bleeding heart

Everyone has seen this native wildflower's showy Japanese relative, *Dicentra spectabilis*, with its bold foliage and plump, locket-shaped flowers in white and pink. Where that plant shouts, this one whispers. Wild bleeding heart takes up just as much space but with more grace and subtlety. Its softer-textured, fernlike foliage carries slender, arching wands laden with inch-long (2.5cm) flowers in a soft shade of pink or mauve. Generally a very agreeable plant, this species does best in rich soil. Exposure is key—too much sun causes the leaves to yellow.

One important quality in which wild bleeding heart excels over its showier cousin is its especially long blooming period. In fact, it is one of the few plants, wild or cultivated, that can be relied upon to remain in bloom from early spring to autumn frost.

Gardeners who have discovered the charms of wild bleeding heart like to plant it in masses. With its mounding, broad habit, it is perhaps too large to be called a ground-cover, but groupings emphasize its airy quality. Try a sweep of it under tall deciduous trees, along a woodland path, at the foot of a rock wall, or in any shaded spot that would benefit from prolific and continual color. Of course, individual plants are welcome in a shady rock garden or shady perennial border.

Diphylleia cymosa

Umbrella-leaf

BLOOM TIME: spring

HEIGHT/WIDTH: 1'–3' × 1'–4' (30–90cm × 30cm–1.2m)

LIGHT: partial–full shade

ZONES: 6–9

Umbrella-leaf

This aptly named woodlander is an adventurous choice for a shade garden. The lobed leaves, carried in pairs, can grow impressively large, up to 20 inches (51cm) across. The flowers, which appear in early spring, are completely upstaged; they are a small cluster of white blooms that don't tend to last very long. However, splendid dark blue berries follow in late summer. Borne aloft on reddish stems, they make a dramatic sight.

Umbrella-leaf has only one stringent requirement—it must have moist soil. The wetter it is, the faster the plant will grow, so site it with care, depending on your plans. It makes nice colonies in humusy soil under the high shade of deciduous trees. For a textured green carpet, intersperse it among ferns or astilbes. You may grow it with other wildflowers, but choose ones that won't be hidden by it. An appropriate big companion is bugbane (*Cimicifuga*).

Dodecatheon meadia

Shooting star

BLOOM TIME: spring

HEIGHT/WIDTH: 6"–20" × 8"–12" (15–51cm × 20–30cm)

LIGHT: full sun–partial shade

ZONES: 4–9

Shooting star

This spring bloomer can travel in two worlds: it is a fine addition to an informal garden along with other wildflowers, but is also at ease in the company of formal tulips, hyacinths, and so forth. In either case, though, the moments of pleasure are to be savored, because shooting star dies back and goes dormant come summer.

The rosettes, composed of light green, paddle-shaped leaves, have a tidy appearance. A slender, leafless stalk rises up from the middle and bears a cluster of dangling little "stars." It is an unusual flower, with swept-back petals and a tiny, pointed, banded cone in the middle. The color varies from purple to lavender to white, and you may have some of each if you plant in quantity.

Shooting star performs well in light shade or even full sun. Its main requirement is for ample soil moisture, at least while it is in bloom. It is appealing in great sweeps—which you'll get over the years as it gradually self-sows. If you manage to match its bloom time with other spring favorites, you are in for a treat.

Echinacea purpurea

Purple coneflower

BLOOM TIME: summer

HEIGHT/WIDTH: 2'–4' × 1'–2' (60cm–1.2m × 30–60cm)

LIGHT: full sun

ZONES: 3–8

Purple coneflower

This native of the North American prairies is widely popular: perennial gardeners prize its good looks and easy care, and herbalists value it for its medicinal qualities (it has a reputation for boosting the immune system, to fight the common cold).

Its big, splendid blooms have especially long petals, up to 2½ inches (6cm), and are generally light purple; the orange to bronze "cone" in the center of each is symmetrical and very prominent. Often the petals droop downward from the cone, giving the plants a whimsical appearance and providing a welcoming stage for visiting butterflies. Carried in great numbers on a coarse, well-branched plant, these blooms make for wonderful bouquets, and flower arrangers love to collect and dry them for the central cones alone—though if you leave them be, the plant tends to self-sow and add to your display with each passing year.

All this hardy plant requires is conditions that match what it thrives on in nature: full sun and average, not overly rich, soil. Purple coneflower develops a substantial root system and deep taproot, so moving and dividing is not recommended. However, this means it will weather periods of drought well and contribute many years of beauty to your garden.

Epilobium angustifolium

Fireweed

BLOOM TIME: summer

HEIGHT/WIDTH: 2'–6' × 2'–3' (60cm–1.8m × 60–90cm)

LIGHT: full sun

ZONES: 3–8

Fireweed

After the great fires in Yellowstone National Park several years ago, this plucky, beautiful wildflower was one of the first plants to begin growing on the ravaged ground. It also grows wild in Europe—it appeared in great numbers around London after the bombings of World War II. In any event, it gets its name from this ability, which advertises its preference for open ground in full sun.

A tall plant, fireweed has striking purple or rosy pink flowers that line the upper portion of the graceful, unbranched stems, the lower ones opening first. They are centered prettily by white stamens and produce lots of nectar for visiting bees (the resulting honey is excellent). When the flowers pass, fluffy seeds gather, then blow away. If you don't want the plant to spread, be sure to deadhead!

Plant fireweed at the back of your borders or along a fence, where it can gain a little support from adjacent plants while interjecting its pretty blooms. If you have the space, try combining it with plants of similar habit, such as *Crocosmia* 'Lucifer', gaura, or dierama.

Eryngium yuccifolium

Rattlesnake master

BLOOM TIME: summer

HEIGHT/WIDTH: 1'–6' × 1'–3' (30cm–1.8m × 30–90cm)

LIGHT: full sun

ZONES: 5–8

Rattlesnake master

Gardeners in mild climates, with dry, infertile soil, may find this to be an intriguing alternative to the ubiquitous yucca. Like yucca, rattlesnake master forms a clump of long, sharp-pointed, and parallel-veined leaves. But the plant generally is not as large as the yucca. Still, you may fool your neighbors until the plant blooms.

A tall flowering stem emerges from the center of the plant, just as it does with the yucca, but the blooms could not be more different. They appear in a small cluster, each button-shaped bloom less than an inch (2.5cm) in diameter.

The flowers are pale green at first, but over time they take on a bluish tinge. The texture is hard and spiny. Be sure to cut them off before they go to seed, or you may have more than you bargained for the next year. Better yet, pick them when they are fully open and they will dry well (retaining their color) for use in dried flower arrangements.

The odd name comes from an old medicinal use. It was believed that a tea made from the root was an effective antidote to rattlesnake bites.

Erythronium spp.

Trout lily

BLOOM TIME: spring

HEIGHT/WIDTH: 5"–12" × 5"–12" (12–30cm × 12–30cm)

LIGHT: partial shade

ZONES: 4–8

Trout lily

Trout lilies probably get their whimsical name from their distinctive foliage; each plant sports just two simple, lance-shaped leaves, mottled or speckled with brown, purple, or even cream markings. One botanist suggests that the other common name, "fawn lily," is inspired by their resemblance to the perked-up ears of a young deer.

The bloom rises above the pair of leaves on slender, wiry stems. It's a pretty thing, between 1 and 3 inches (2.5–7cm) across and looking very much like a nodding, slightly flared lily flower (the plant is in the same family as cultivated lilies). The flowers of *E. americanum* are chiffon yellow brushed with chocolate brown marks. Because those

of the enchanting *E. revolutum* vary from rosy pink to soft pink to white, selections were inevitable. 'Rose Beauty' and 'White Beauty' are available from bulb suppliers and specialty nurseries. But perhaps the most popular cultivar, apparently derived from *E. tuolumnense*, is the sunny yellow 'Pagoda'. Its flowers and leaves are much larger than those of the others, and it is an eager, robust grower.

The best place for trout lilies is high, open shade under deciduous trees. The soil should be organically rich and well drained. Because they go dormant after blooming, you may wish to overplant with other shade-tolerant plants.

Eschscholzia californica

California poppy

BLOOM TIME: summer

HEIGHT/WIDTH: 6"–12" × 6"–12" (15–30cm × 15–30cm)

LIGHT: full sun

ZONES: all zones (annual)

California poppy

Anyone who has seen a California hillside or meadow strewn with these deep orange flowers never forgets it. Up close, the flowers look a bit frail; they are composed of four silky petals that splay outward (and drop not long after being picked). They do fold up each evening, a habit that led early Spanish explorers to dub it "dormidera," the drowsy one.

California poppy is an annual, a cinch to raise from seeds sown each spring (in milder climates, it will self-sow for you in subsequent years). As its native habitat suggests, it prospers in lean soil in full sun. In recent years, seed catalogs have been offering alternative colors, including lemon yellow, crimson, bicolors, and mixes. 'Apricot Flambeau' is exotic-looking, with fluted petals and semidouble form.

The foliage deserves praise, too. It is a wonderful shade of gray-green, ferny and lacy, and almost succulent in texture. It can be a bit sprawling, especially late in the season, but this is a virtue if you are growing the plants among other flowers as a "weaver."

Eupatorium fistulosum

Joe-Pye weed

BLOOM TIME: summer–autumn

HEIGHT/WIDTH: 4'–8' × 2'–4' (1.2–2.4m × 60cm–1.2m)

LIGHT: full sun–partial shade

ZONES: 4–8

Joe-Pye weed

Here is another North American wildflower that has gained appreciation in the gardens of Europe but is still underused in its native land. It's a shame, because, in the right spot, Joe-Pye weed is both magnificent and utterly dependable.

This is a large, imposing plant, best used in informal groups at the back of the border or as a perennial screen. It does well in sun and part shade alike, prefers damp soil, and blooms best when it gets enough moisture. The flowers appear later in the summer, and they are worth the wait: they foam forth in clusters of rose-pink to light purple, waft a sweet, enticing fragrance, and draw butterflies.

The erect but hollow stems are wine-red and very robust — they remain standing after late-summer storms while other garden plants are smashed down. They are clothed in handsome, toothed leaves that may be as long as a foot (30cm).

Joe-Pye weed is also available in other sizes and colors. The most popular is 'Gateway', a handsome hybrid between this species and the similar *E. maculatum*; it features darker, reddish purple blooms and is not as tall.

Filipendula rubra

Queen-of-the-prairie

BLOOM TIME: summer

HEIGHT/WIDTH: 6'–8' × 3'–4' (1.8–2.4m × 1–1.2m)

LIGHT: full sun–partial shade

ZONES: 3–9

Queen-of-the-prairie

A towering, bushy beauty, this plant has elegant flower plumes up to 9 inches (23cm) long. They're composed of myriad tiny pink flowers. Deadheading will prolong the already generous blooming period. (Alas, the flowers don't hold up well in a vase, but they can be dried for use in wreaths and swags.) The flowers are joined by jagged, forest-green leaves that clothe especially strong stems; the plant stands up well to wind and weather.

Queen-of-the-prairie is not a dryland plant, despite what the name may suggest. In nature, it grows in damp or even wet soil in meadows and wetlands, and you must give it the same if you want it to thrive. Try it in a poorly drained spot such as along a back stone wall or fence. Sometimes water gardeners border the far side of their pools with it, with spectacular results.

A wildflower this handsome and long-blooming has not escaped the notice of nurserymen. You can find 'Venusta', with deep rose-pink blooms, the related *F. ulmaria* 'Variegata', with white flowers and yellow-dappled leaves, and—if the species is just too big for your garden—a dwarf one called 'Nana', which grows to only 15 inches (38cm) tall.

Gaillardia pulchella

Indian blanket, blanket flower

BLOOM TIME: summer

HEIGHT/WIDTH: 1'–2' × 1'–2' (30–60cm × 30–60cm)

LIGHT: full sun

ZONES: all zones (annual)

Indian blanket

You probably know this bright wildflower's perennial cousin, which also goes by the name of Indian blanket, *Gaillardia* × *grandiflora*. That species has a number of popular cultivars, most notably the red-and-yellow 'Goblin'. *G. pulchella* also has seen the hand of the horticulturist—the cultivar 'Red Plume' was an All-America selections winner back in 1991. 'Red Plume' is a fabulous wine-red through and through, and so full of petals that to call it "double" would be an understatement. In fact, the flower looks a bit like a mum. It does not look much like its parent, though.

Let's not forget the original Indian blanket, which is a worthy garden subject in its own right. Although it is native to fields and roadsides of the southeastern United States, it can be grown almost anywhere. As you might expect from its native habitat, it is sun-loving and drought-tolerant. Best of all, as an annual, it will give you great color immediately—and, at season's end, it will self-sow.

In the manner of many wild species, this Indian blanket's flowers show a fair amount of variation. The jagged-edged petals may be scarlet, red, or russet, may contain stripes of gold or warm orange, and are usually tipped yellow. Sometimes a patch will produce a few solid-color individuals. The effect is exciting, as vibrant and colorful as an Indian saddle blanket.

Galax urceolata

(G. aphylla)

Galax

BLOOM TIME: spring

HEIGHT/WIDTH: 8"–20" × 6"–12" (20–51cm × 15–30cm)

LIGHT: partial shade

ZONES: 5 or 6–8

Galax

If you have a damp spot in shade in your yard, here is the groundcovering plant that will change the site from a problem into a spectacle. And unlike other plants that enjoy these conditions, like certain mints or gooseneck loosestrife, galax will not become an invasive weed.

The plant's best asset is its lovely, leafless wands of tiny white flowers, which appear every spring and last for several weeks. A group planting becomes enchanting. But the leaves are also attractive, and you will appreciate them long after the flowers have passed. They are glossy green, sometimes tinged russet, rounded, and leathery, so they hold up well through the dog days of summer. They also make nice greenery for bouquets or holiday decorations because they are long-lasting. (In the plant's native Appalachian forests, unfortunately, stands have been plundered for these purposes.)

Gaura lindheimeri

Gaura

BLOOM TIME: summer

HEIGHT/WIDTH: 3'–4' × 1'–3' (1–1.2m × 30–90cm)

LIGHT: full sun

ZONES: 5–9

Gaura

All summer long, gaura is a fountain of lovely, delicate-looking white flowers that age to a pretty shade of light, rosy pink. (The harder-to-find species *G. coccinea* features scarlet blooms.) These are carried on the upper part of long, willowy stems. The leaves, which are dark to medium green and spear-shaped, tend to remain low on the plant and not steal the show.

To give of its best, gaura really deserves a place out in the open or a spot in the flower border with room to spread out. It is a wonderful weaver, gently inserting its butterfly-like blooms among the upright stems of taller perennials or flowering shrubs. Try gaura near pink or white roses; you'll appreciate how it softens the stiff uprightness of their canes.

Established gaura plants have a sturdy, fleshy root (like a carrot) and are quite drought-tolerant, but well-drained soil is still an important requirement. Gardeners in the hot, humid South are especially enthusiastic about this terrific plant. It will still do well up north, but may not bloom until later in the summer in cooler areas.

Gentiana andrewsii

Bottle gentian

BLOOM TIME: late summer

HEIGHT/WIDTH: 1'–2' × 6"–12" (30–60cm × 15–30cm)

LIGHT: full sun–partial shade

ZONES: 4–9

Bottle gentian

One of the easiest wildflowers to grow is the curious and beautiful bottle, or closed, gentian. The color is brilliant blue, even more appreciated because the flowers appear in clusters of three to twelve. And the shape is unique—bottle gentian flowers never open fully, but hold their petals closed in a more or less cylindrical shape. There are several plausible explanations for this: it helps keep the pollen dry as the autumn rainy season begins, it permits self-pollination, or it offers late-in-the-year bees shelter if they are visiting the flower and the temperature drops.

In any event, you need not worry about the viability of your bottle gentian plants. They grow easily from seed (though they delay bloom until their second year), transplant readily, can be successfully divided, and are long-lived. They are easy garden subjects, asking only for the moist, rich soil they enjoy in wild meadows and along stream banks. They can grow in some shade, but bloom more profusely in full sun.

As for color combinations with bottle gentian, other primary colors are particularly good choices, such as the cultivated goldenrods or scarlet cardinal flower. If you grow bottle gentian in a shadier spot, ferns make natural and delightful companions.

Geranium maculatum

Wild geranium

BLOOM TIME: spring

HEIGHT/WIDTH: 1'–2' × 10"–12" (30–60cm × 25–30cm)

LIGHT: partial shade–full sun

ZONES: 4–9

Wild geranium

If you already have this plant in your garden, you probably take it for granted. It seems to thrive, and spread, with little or no attention from the gardener. Wild geranium is closely related to many popular cranesbill geraniums, such as 'Johnson's Blue' and 'Claridge Druce'. Its leaves are similar, that is, deeply indented. Unlike those plants, however, its magenta-pink flowers are about an inch (2.5cm) across (the blooms are admittedly small, but not as tiny as those of its weedy cousin, an herb known as Robert [*G. robertianum*]). There is also a lovely white-flowered cultivar called 'Album'.

The plant spreads as its creeping rhizome expands outward. It also self-sows—the beaklike pod matures black and bursts open to hurl seeds in all directions. So once you have this geranium, you will never lack for more. Fortunately, colonies of this perky plant are quite appealing. And if you want to contain it, simply tear out the unwanted plants.

Wild geranium can also be added to a fern glade to good effect. It will weave among the greenery, poking up its bright flowers here and there. It also naturalizes nicely at the bases of trees. Just remember that prolonged dry spells will cause it to go dormant for the rest of the season.

Geum triflorum

Prairie smoke

BLOOM TIME: spring

HEIGHT/WIDTH: 6"–15" × 6"–15" (15–38cm × 15–38cm)

LIGHT: full sun–partial shade

ZONES: 2–7

Prairie smoke

On the prairies of the Midwest, this enchanting wildflower is one of the earliest plants to bloom. The flowers consist of small but stout rosy pink nodding bracts clasped by purplish sepals (the true petals are light brown and hidden within). They look somewhat like fat, unopened rosebuds, and, in fact, the plant is in the rose family. But that's where the resemblance ends.

The seedheads that follow in early summer are what give this unique plant its common name. The flowers ultimately do spring open (once pollinated) and puffs of tiny, slender, soft pink plumes ("smoke") emanate. When the plants are grown in a drift, the effect is enchanting.

The clumping foliage, which is not at all roselike, turns russet or crimson in autumn. It is long and irregularly lobed, a bit like coarser yarrow foliage. Prairie smoke is well able to compete with grasses, so feel free to interplant with your favorite ornamental types, or sedges. The creeping phloxes that also bloom in early spring in pink, lavender, or white *(P. subulata* or *P. bifida)* are nice companions as well.

Grow this stalwart in average or even poor soil, provided it is well drained. If prairie smoke is happy, it will eventually form a large colony. You can dig up and move pieces, but be sure to get a good chunk of the rhizome.

Helianthus annuus

Sunflower

BLOOM TIME: summer

HEIGHT/WIDTH: 3'–12' × 2'–5' (1–3.5m × 60cm–1.5m)

LIGHT: full sun

ZONES: all zones (annual)

Sunflower

Contrary to what you may have assumed from Van Gogh's famous paintings of the French countryside, the sunflower is native to North America. The exchange between the Old World and the New was not even—there are many more European imports to the United States than the reverse. But perhaps the bold golden splendor of this plant tips the scales somewhat.

Of course, a plant this easy to grow and of such dramatic form was quickly seized upon by horticulturists. Some domesticated versions have flower heads more than 12 inches (30cm) wide. The original annual species can be as small as 6 inches (15cm) to 10 inches (25cm) across and has pale yellow petals ("ray flowers"). It has parented a great range of color choices, from the warm red 'Velvet Queen' to the creamy white 'Italian White', and everything in between. In recent years, seed companies have touted towering ones (Burpee sells one called 'Paul Bunyan' that can reach 15 feet [4.5m] tall!) and dwarf ones with jumbo flowers ('Teddy Bear'). It is amazing to realize that all of these annual sunflowers really do go from a small seed to mature size in just a few months. Just be sure to provide all the rich soil and water they need.

Heracleum maximum

(H. sphondylium ssp. montanum)

Cow parsnip

BLOOM TIME: summer

HEIGHT/WIDTH: 4'–10' × 3'–5' (1.2–3m × 1–1.5m)

LIGHT: partial sun

ZONES: 6–8

Cow parsnip

This is one of those plants that causes garden visitors to pause and, after a moment's consideration, exclaim, "Wow! What is that?" It has strong, stout, hollow stems and grows as tall as its relative fennel, with divided, maplelike leaves in threes. Its numerous white, flat-topped umbel flowers, which appear in the second season, are similar to those of many garden herbs and to cultivated parsnip—though they can be enormous, up to 8 inches (20cm) across.

Native to moist, shady spots such as wooded stream banks, cow parsnip prefers similar conditions in the garden, such as a damp back corner, a site on the north or east side of the house or garage, or as a backdrop for a water garden or boggy spot. The large white flower heads are a sensational way to light up dreary areas.

Once considered too large or weedy for gardens, cow parsnip has enjoyed the recent praise of trendy gardeners seeking ever larger and more surprising plant choices. When you give it the conditions it requires, you can count on cow parsnip to provide big drama.

Heuchera americana

Alumroot

BLOOM TIME: late spring

HEIGHT/WIDTH: 2'–3' × 8"–12" (60–90cm × 20–30cm)

LIGHT: full sun–partial shade

ZONES: 5–8

Alumroot

The handsome foliage on this low-growing plant will remind you of maple leaves. Alumroot's leaves begin the year apple green highlighted by darker veins, develop silvery tints or splashes as summer arrives, and change by autumn to russet or bronze (especially in sunnier locations). At 2 to 5 inches (5 to 13cm) across, the leaves are often smaller than some of the fancier garden heucheras, making the plant more useful for rock gardens and tight spaces. Rather tall, slender wands of miniature green or lavender bell-shaped flowers rise above the rosette in late spring and last for a few weeks; they are pretty but, because of their delicacy, not reason enough to grow this plant.

Use alumroot in a spot where its quiet good looks make it a supporting player to spring bulbs or smaller flowering perennials. It also makes a nice groundcover in sun or filtered shade, particularly in combination with ferns. All it needs is rich, fertile soil that drains well. Divide it every few years or when it becomes woody in the center. In mild-climate areas, it should be evergreen over the winter.

Hibiscus moscheutos

Rose mallow

BLOOM TIME: summer

HEIGHT/WIDTH: 3'–6' × 3'–6' (1–1.8m × 1–1.8m)

LIGHT: full sun

ZONES: 5–9

Rose mallow

Bigger and hardier than the familiar houseplant hibiscus (*H. rosa-sinensis*) but smaller and more herbaceous than rose-of-Sharon (*H. syriacus*), this native North American plant may be just the hibiscus for your garden beds. It grows quickly and lustily, with a shrubby profile and enormous, attractive flowers.

The species is white with a crimson eye, but there are many cultivated varieties in the pink and red range, with and without contrasting eyes. The flower form is what you would expect, but the size is impressive. Often the blooms are 6 to 8 inches (15 to 20cm) across, though some are up to 15 inches (38cm) across (prompting the catalog cliché, "flowers as big as dinner plates!"). If this strikes your fancy, look for the Southern Belle strain, the Disco Belle strain, or, the biggest of them all, white-flowered 'Blue River II'.

The maplelike foliage provides a nice green backdrop, and generally cloaks the plant from head to toe. So probably the best uses of rose mallow are as a foundation plant or an informal hedge. It doesn't mind average soil but needs consistent moisture, especially during the heat of summer. Just one caveat: like other mallows, this plant is vulnerable to nibbling Japanese beetles.

Iris cristata

Dwarf crested iris

BLOOM TIME: spring

HEIGHT/WIDTH: 4"–12" × 2"–4" (10–30cm × 5–10cm)

LIGHT: full sun–partial shade

ZONES: 5–8

'Alba' dwarf crested iris

This is a special iris for special spots. Unlike some of its kin, it prefers lean, well-drained, even dry soils. Too much moisture makes it pump out foliage at the expense of flowers, and fertilizer is not necessary. Its petite size makes it suitable for places where larger irises might never be used—try it as an edging bordering a walkway or wall, tuck it into a rock garden, or plant it at the feet of taller plants. Dwarf crested iris does best in ground that drains well, as mentioned above, so a slope or bank might also be a good site. In any event, plant the fleshy roots very near the surface. Over the years, if the plants are happy, they will form a dense patch. Fortunately, this iris is not susceptible to the dreaded iris borer, which can devastate the fancy cultivated varieties.

The lightly scented flowers may be small, but they display plenty of perky color. Petals are marked with royal purple and lavender; the "crest" is yellow and white. (Some wildflower nurseries offer the rare and lovely 'Alba', which is white with a golden crest.) Bladelike, light green leaves carry on the show after the blooms pass; their little tufts, growing en masse, are quite attractive.

Iris pseudacorus

Yellow flag

BLOOM TIME: spring–summer

HEIGHT/WIDTH: 3' × 2'–3' (90cm × 60–90cm)

LIGHT: full sun

ZONES: 4–9

Yellow flag

This is a showy plant for damp to outright wet soils, though it will also grow in ordinary soil. In nature, it skirts wetlands and pond edges, making a striking sight each spring with scores of bright yellow blooms. These are of good size, 3 to 4 inches (7 to 10cm) across.

As with all irises, the stiff, sword-shaped, slightly bluish foliage is handsome when the plant is out of bloom. A variegated one, 'Variegata', has cream-striped leaves that are really gorgeous—splendid in combination with the flowers, a standout in the garden at any time, and a great mixer with many other perennials.

This plant is described in some plant catalogs as "vigorous," which is true. It might be more accurate to say "aggressive," because it self-sows eagerly, especially if you give it a wet area. You can keep it in check over the years by yanking out unwanted clumps. The tall British cultivar 'Roy Davidson' is supposed to be sterile, so it might be a better choice if you want to contain your yellow iris.

Iris versicolor

Blue flag

BLOOM TIME: late spring–early summer

HEIGHT/WIDTH: 1'–3' × 8"–12" (30–90cm × 20–30cm)

LIGHT: full sun

ZONES: 2–9

Blue flag

There are plenty of highly bred, beautiful irises in the world, but there is still something to be said for the good old wild species, blue flag. It is very tough, very hardy, and very low-maintenance, qualities some of its fancier descendants and relatives have lost along the way. It grows in damp areas in nature, and prefers the same in your garden.

The flowers, which measure a modest 4 inches (10cm) or so across, are usually a nice robin's-egg blue, with sunny yellow veins. (Interestingly, these veins have a practical purpose. They guide pollinating bees to the interior of the flower—sort of the same theory as runway lights, if you will.) The flat, pale green to grayish leaves are well in scale with the rest of the plant, at ½ inch to 1 inch (1 to 2.5cm) wide.

In nature, the large rhizomes are evident just below the soil line or maybe emerging slightly from it; you should recreate this condition when planting it in your garden—blue flag that is planted too deeply grows poorly and may be subject to rot. Over the years, a rhizome will elongate, producing lots of leaves and quite a few flowering stalks, so in time it will look like you have a clump of blue flag plants when you really have only one.

Jeffersonia diphylla

Twinleaf

BLOOM TIME: spring

HEIGHT/WIDTH: 8"–10" × 6" (20–25cm × 15cm)

LIGHT: partial shade

ZONES: 5–7

Twinleaf

Thomas Jefferson, as you probably know, was a keen gardener, and not only nurtured plants of all kinds (natives as well as European ones), but also supported the botanists and horticulturists of his day. It is somewhat curious, then, that this quirky North American woodlander is the only genus named in his honor.

The blue-green, red-rimmed foliage, which inspired its species name, *diphylla*, looks like a matched set but turns out to be one large but almost completely divided heart-shaped leaf. One writer describes the leaves as "unfurling as if in prayer," another likens them to "bird's wings poised for flight." Since each plant bears about four leaves, the effect is rather busy. A carpet of twinleaf makes for a real conversation piece, no doubt about it.

The 1-inch (2.5cm) creamy white, eight-petaled flower that appears for a short time in early spring looks like a small bloodroot blossom. Like bloodroot, each plant bears only one, held proudly aloft on a slender, bare stem. Later in the season, you can observe the odd, pear-shaped fruit, which opens with a hinged lid to reveal a full load of tiny, chestnut brown seeds, ready to spread this unique plant. Humus-rich soil inspires the best growth and appearance.

Liatris spicata

Blazing star

BLOOM TIME: summer

HEIGHT/WIDTH: 2'–5' × 18" (60cm–1.5m × 45cm)

LIGHT: full sun

ZONES: 3–9

'Kobold' blazing star

Treasured by butterfly lovers as well as bouquet pickers, blazing star is a champ. It blooms eagerly, bearing wonderful, dense spires of small, usually purple flowers (interestingly, unlike most spike flowers, the top ones open first, then the show proceeds downward). These are carried one-to-a-stem, making harvesting easy. They last a long time in a vase, and dry well, too. But if you can bear to leave them growing, your wildflower garden will soon be hosting flitting butterflies.

A native of the North American prairies, blazing star is a tough plant. It does best in somewhat sandy, fertile soil, and develops a strong tuberous rootstock that stores water for survival during dry spells.

A number of excellent cultivars have been developed from the species. The popular 'Kobold' is shorter, around 2 feet (60cm) tall, and has dark reddish purple blooms. 'Floristan White' has gorgeous pure white spikes.

Lilium canadense

Meadow lily

BLOOM TIME: summer

HEIGHT/WIDTH: 2'–7' × 1'–2' (60cm–2m × 30–60cm)

LIGHT: full sun–partial shade

ZONES: 3–8

Meadow lily

The great thing about the big-flowered Asiatic and Oriental lilies is their uniformity. The great thing about wild species lilies like this one is their variability. The blooms of meadow lily begin as orange buds and flare open to sunny yellow on the outsides of the petals and orange with stippled maroon marks within. Usually. Sometimes, the entire flower is more yellow, sometimes more orange. While some are open, others are still in bud. They are a cheerful sight — brighter and more spontaneous, it seems, than their fancy cultivated cousins.

Meadow lily, as you might guess, likes meadow conditions — that is, full sun and damp soil. It will grow in part-day shade, too, as long as the soil is wet. There is no need to fertilize or otherwise fuss over the plants. Once established, they will bloom lustily every summer for a few weeks.

Keep in mind, however, the size of this lily. It is a tall one, with sturdy stalks, and when well-situated, will end up being taller than the gardener. A single plant, or a small grouping, is a nice choice for the back of a border. Or grow a clump at the edge of a wooded area of your property.

Lilium superbum

Turk's-cap lily

BLOOM TIME: summer

HEIGHT/WIDTH: 3'–7' × 1'–2' (90cm–2m × 30–60cm)

LIGHT: full sun–partial shade

ZONES: 4–9

Turk's-cap lily

This is not a lily for the fainthearted. It towers above most gardeners, displaying dozens of 5-inch (13cm), nodding, orange to red flowers on the upper reaches of its stout stems. These, as the whimsical common name suggests, are "highly reflexed," meaning they curl back almost completely to display the spotted surface of the bright petals, the green throat, and the dangling stamens. The tall habit of Turk's-cap lily is a good thing, then, because you can stand under the plant, look up, and admire the details of these exquisite blooms.

The plant looks best in small groupings. Over the years, it will send out thick runners that generate new little bulbs and, shortly, more plants.

To put on a stellar performance, Turk's-cap lily should be planted in rich, moisture-retentive (but not perpetually soggy) soil, conditions it enjoys in wild meadows. Full sun all day long is not absolutely necessary; some gardeners grow it along a fence or wall that provides a few hours of afternoon shade and some shelter from the wind. Although the stalks are strong, a summer storm can flatten them.

Lobelia cardinalis

Cardinal flower

BLOOM TIME: mid–late summer

HEIGHT/WIDTH: 3'–5' × 1' (1–1.5m × 30cm)

LIGHT: full sun–full shade

ZONES: 2–9

Cardinal flower

This is one of the very best wildflowers for garden use, thanks to its agreeable disposition and beautiful flowers. In nature, cardinal flower appears in damp meadows and along streams, so you can grow it in a damp spot. Lacking that, however, it will be happy with regular watering and a mulch at its feet to preserve soil moisture.

A robust plant, yet not rangy or invasive, cardinal flower has striking flower spires. Perhaps no more than 1½ inches (4cm) long, each blossom has the distinctive fan-like shape you may have observed in the common blue garden lobelias so popular for edgings and window boxes.

The species is scarlet, but variations can be found if you hunt for them (some may be crosses with other, similar, lobelias). 'Ruby Slippers' is an especially gorgeous choice, as is the richly hued, more subtle 'Garnet'. There is also a white ('Alba'), a soft pink ('Heather Pink'), a hot pink ('Pink Parade'), and many others. These are carried on tall stalks that emerge from a low rosette. The leaves are medium to dark green, oblong, and slightly serrated, and they ascend the stalk to just short of the blooms. You can count on cardinal flower to grace either flower borders or wildflower beds for many weeks later in the season.

Lobelia siphilitica

Great blue lobelia

BLOOM TIME: late summer

HEIGHT/WIDTH: 2'–4' × 8"–12" (60cm–1.2cm ×
20–30cm)

LIGHT: full sun–partial shade

ZONES: 6–9

Great blue lobelia

Even gardeners who like the closely related cardinal flower don't always know this wonderful wildflower. But a few nurseries specializing in native plants carry it, and it comes recommended highly. It tolerates less moisture and direct sun better than cardinal flower.

Somewhat shorter than its cousin, great blue lobelia has multibranched stems. The flowers are slightly smaller, and range from periwinkle blue to pale blue—occasionally, a white one appears. They are a pretty sight accompanied by the mint green foliage.

A natural use would be to plant it together with cardinal flower's scarlet blooms—a sweep devoted to them alone would be stunning. But if you want to capitalize on the elegance of its bloom color, try some around a white flower such as 'Snow Queen' bee balm, or combine it with another pastel, like pink obedient plant.

Lupinus perennis

Lupine

BLOOM TIME: late spring–early summer

HEIGHT/WIDTH: 8"–2' × 8"–18" (20–60cm × 20–45cm)

LIGHT: full sun

ZONES: 4–7

Lupine

Lucky residents of Maine have seen and adored the great sweeps that this blue wildflower makes in spring in open fields and road banks. The wild lupine is often easier to grow in the garden than some of its more refined relatives that blaze across the colorful pages of nursery catalogs. Its main requirement is well-drained soil. And you will have better luck if you start with smaller seedlings—seeds may germinate erratically (though presoaking them helps), while larger plants transplant poorly, thanks to their deep root systems.

The racemes are light blue with a touch of purple within, and can be as long as 10 inches (25cm). The plant holds them erect, but the foliage tends to be sprawling, so wild lupine is probably not a good candidate for showcasing in a formal perennial border. Better to take your cue from nature and plant it en masse, perhaps in an area where grass is thin. For companions, try other hardy wildflowers with bright flowers, such as butterfly weed. Unlike the hybrids, this species is long-lived.

Lythrum salicaria

Purple loosestrife

BLOOM TIME: late summer

HEIGHT/WIDTH: 3'–4' × 2'–3' (90cm–1.2m × 60–90cm)

LIGHT: full sun

ZONES: 4–9

Purple loosestrife

Possibly the most controversial wildflower of recent years, purple loosestrife is both lovely to look at and, according to its detractors, a dangerous weed. It is native to Europe and Asia; its fast-sprouting seeds were originally brought to North America by early settlers, inadvertently in either ship ballast or livestock bedding. It wasn't long before the seeds "escaped" and became a pest in wetlands and roadside ditches, and along streambanks.

Nonetheless, present-day gardeners have been susceptible to the plant's bright color and long bloom period, so welcome in late summer and early autumn. Like any self-respecting weed, purple loosestrife is widely adaptable, and will grow well in most soils (provided it gets the moisture it needs). Cultivated varieties have been introduced by the nursery trade, among them the gorgeous pink 'Morden Pink' and 'Rosy Queen'. Allegedly, these produce sterile seeds, though research has challenged this.

And therein lies the problem. Fertile purple loosestrife seed of any kind has come to be regarded as a menace by botanists. A number of states with overrun wetlands agree and have banned the sale of purple loosestrife plants. If it is not illegal to grow it in your state, and you've fallen in love with the beautiful flowers, plant it well away from any wild wet areas and deadhead the blooms before they go to seed.

Mertensia virginica

Bluebells

BLOOM TIME: spring

HEIGHT/WIDTH: 1'–2' × 18" (30–60cm × 45cm)

LIGHT: partial–full shade

ZONES: 3–9

Virginia bluebells

A native of southeastern woodlands but able to grow well much further north, bluebells is a pretty plant. The thin, lance-shaped leaves are mainly basal, though a few ascend the stems on short, succulent stalks. At the top of these stalks are clusters of nodding little bells. They begin as pink buds, but open to lilac-blue flowers. The blue will be darker in deeper shade.

Bluebells are often touted as ideal companions for spring-flowering bulbs, with good reason. This plant likes similar conditions in the garden: organically rich soil in cool shade. Plus, the color seems to go with everything. It is particularly fetching combined with small-flowered yellow or white narcissus.

Like the bulbs, though, bluebells' show ends as summer arrives. The stems die down after bloom, and the plant gradually goes dormant and disappears from view, until the next year. So mark its spot if you wish to move or divide it in the autumn, and to avoid trampling on it or planting something else over it.

Mimulus spp.

Monkey flower

BLOOM TIME: summer

HEIGHT/WIDTH: 1'–4' × 8"–3' (30cm–1.2m × 20–90cm)

LIGHT: full sun

ZONES: 5–7

Monkey flower

The charming, long-blooming flowers look something like a monkey face, hence the common name (amusingly, legend has it that the Latin name refers to a mime actor, Mimus; apparently the word means "buffoon"). There are many species of this wetland wildflower, of varying sizes. Many have yellow flowers, including *M. luteus*, *M. moschatus*, and *M. guttatus*; *M. cardinalis* 'Aurantiacus' has rich orangey flowers. Those of *M. lewisii* are rosy pink. And a monkey flower from the Appalachians, *M. ringens*, is light purple (and, rarely, white).

Whichever ones you choose, be sure to give them damp or constantly wet soil. Because monkey flower plants have a tendency to spread over time, they are a good choice for a boggy area or the perimeter of a water garden. Just remember, if they dry out, you will lose them. Otherwise, they require little attention from the gardener in exchange for many weeks of colorful and intriguing bloom.

Monarda didyma

Bee balm

BLOOM TIME: mid–late summer

HEIGHT/WIDTH: 2'6"–3' × 18' (75–90cm × 45cm)

LIGHT: full sun–partial shade

ZONES: 4–9

Bee balm

This showy wildflower is easy to grow, provided your garden has the rich, moist soil it needs to thrive. It has dark green aromatic leaves, and the big flower heads, up to 4 inches (10cm) across, are a knockout in full bloom. Hummingbirds find them irresistible, and you can expect bees, too, of course.

The original species is reddish, but variation in the wild and in gardens is not unusual. So, not surprisingly, there are a number of named color selections. Most often seen is scarlet ('Cambridge Scarlet', 'Gardenview Scarlet'), but recent years have seen a flurry of new introductions in other colors. 'Marshall's Delight' is peppermint pink, 'Aquarius' is rich mauve-pink, 'Vintage Wine' is a deep zinfandel red, and 'Snow Queen' is pure white.

Bee balm can be an overenthusiastic grower; keep it in bounds by chopping back at the outer perimeter of the roots. Traditionally, this stalwart plant has been susceptible to mildew, which disfigures it later in the season. Fortunately, many of the new varieties mentioned above are, while not immune, touted as "resistant." You can also do your part by offering each plant enough elbow room to allow for air circulation, and spraying if need be.

Oenothera spp.

Evening primrose, sundrops

BLOOM TIME: spring–summer

HEIGHT/WIDTH: 2'–3' × 1'–2' (60–90cm × 30–60cm)

LIGHT: full sun

ZONES: 4–9

Sundrops

A number of similar plants gather under these names; all sport tallish stalks laden, near the tops, with sunny yellow, cup-shaped blossoms. Some open true to their name, in the late afternoon or evening (a desirable quality for those who cannot enjoy their gardens until they get home from school or work each day). These are fragrant, to attract night-pollinating moths. Sundrops are those species, notably *O. fruticosa*, that open in the daytime. None are long-lived, but they all self-sow.

The bright color of evening primrose plants is welcome in casual garden settings, where they bloom reliably, prolifically, and practically all summer long. They aren't fussy about soil, though especially fertile ground causes the stems to become lax and floppy. Let their neighbors offer support (penstemons or campanulas are nice companions), or stake them, as the weight of the blooms can sometimes cause them to lean over.

If you grow this wildflower, you should make it a point to sit out with it some evening (or day, as the case may be) and witness a bloom opening, a process that takes about a half an hour. As the tightly rolled, cigar-shaped buds loosen, the sepals peel back, then the petals spring open to reveal the cross-shaped stigma in the center—a show one writer aptly called "reminiscent of time-lapse photography."

Pachysandra procumbens

Allegheny spurge, American pachysandra

BLOOM TIME: spring

HEIGHT/WIDTH: 10"–12" × 10"–12" (25–30cm × 25–30cm)

LIGHT: partial shade

ZONES: 4–9

Allegheny spurge

Everyone knows this native wild plant's famous Japanese relative, the ubiquitous glossy green groundcover (*P. terminalis*); this one looks different and has different requirements. Allegheny spurge is an easy but offbeat groundcover for your damp shade garden.

One significant difference is the growth rate. This pachysandra is not nearly as rampant, instead spreading slowly and judiciously over the years (so yank out invading weeds in its early years). It languishes in the poor, dry soil its cousin performs so well in. To get the best out of Allegheny spurge, grow it in rich, damp soil like the shady woodlands from which it hails.

And the leaves are significantly different. Individually, they are much larger, up to twice as large. In lighter shade, their coloring tends to be gray-green mottled with silver; under heavier cover, they become darker-hued, and the dappling approaches purple-black. This foliage is also more textured, thanks to puckering along the veins, giving the leaves an appealing quilted look. Unfortunately, they are not evergreen, except perhaps in milder areas. As for the flowers, they appear briefly in spring, little lavender to white bottlebrushes with a sweet scent.

Penstemon spp.

Penstemon

BLOOM TIME: summer

HEIGHT/WIDTH: 1'–4' × 1'–3' (30cm–1.2m × 30–90cm)

LIGHT: full sun

ZONES: 6–8

Penstemon

As a group, penstemons are handsome, shrubby-looking plants of arching stems laden with showy, tubular flowers that attract hummingbirds. Many are native to the mountains of the West, but may be grown in other areas, provided similar conditions are available: full sun and lean, well-drained soil (damp or rich soil causes them to rot). Be advised that they are not long-lived, though they may self-sow.

A few of the most popular garden penstemons are the scarlet-flowered *P. barbatus*, white to pale-purple flowered *P. digitalis*, and *P. gloxinioides (P. hartwegii)*, which comes in a variety of colors. Other species are considered tricky and are better left to collectors and rock-garden specialists.

Arguably the best penstemons, though, are the many hybrids and cultivars, which feature the finest qualities of this species—drought tolerance, heavy flowering, and ease of cultivation. Look for the award-winning 'Husker Red', derived from *P. digitalis*, which owes its name to its reddish foliage and stems; the flowers are white, though sometimes they develop a pink cast. This gorgeous plant would make a stunning addition to a low-maintenance border. Well-stocked nurseries will carry, in addition to white-flowered varieties, ones with lavender, violet, blue, pink, true red, and orange-red blooms.

Penstemon smallii

Beard tongue

BLOOM TIME: late spring

HEIGHT/WIDTH: 1½'–3' × 1' (45–90cm × 30cm)

LIGHT: full sun–partial shade

ZONES: 6–8

Beard tongue

There are many penstemons that have traveled from the wild into our gardens, often with no horticultural improvements or selection—with good reason. These are great plants, in the right spot, tough and drought-tolerant and bringing pretty, long-lasting flowers atop attractive, disease-free, noninvasive plants. *Penstemon smallii* is a favorite because the blooms are especially showy—lavender or pink with creamy white throats. Also, they appear down the stems, not just at the tips, so the plant looks bushier than some of its kin.

And what is the right spot? Well, soil seems to be the most important requirement; grow this and most other penstemons in average ground (overly rich soil shortens the life span) that is well drained. Thin or sandy soil is fine, so beard tongue is a good choice for a rock garden, where its taller profile can be a welcome contrast among more sprawling plants. It may also be tucked in among salvias and lavenders, which thrive in similar conditions.

Phacelia campanularia

Desert bluebells

BLOOM TIME: summer

HEIGHT/WIDTH: 6"–20" × 6"–20" (15–51cm × 15–51cm)

LIGHT: full sun–partial shade

ZONES: all zones (annual)

Desert bluebells

The best way to describe the color of these amazing flowers is electric or navy blue, similar to the color of *Salvia guaranitica* flowers, if you know that ornamental sage. These are little bells, about an inch (2.5cm) long, with protruding yellow stamens. They are carried in loose clusters, giving the plant a jaunty, carefree appearance.

Other features of desert bluebells add to its appeal. The heart-shaped leaves are coarsely toothed and clothe the plant well without overwhelming the flower display. And the stems are reddish, which provides nice contrast.

Although it originally hails from dry hillsides and desert areas from Colorado to California, desert bluebells adapts easily to any well-drained soil. In mild climates, an autumn sowing will give you a head start on early blooms the next spring.

Desert bluebells makes a good filler in casual cottage garden designs. This plant is super in the company of the yellow flowers of coreopsis. And you can't go wrong combining it with that sensational annual, bright orange California poppy.

Phlox paniculata

Summer phlox

BLOOM TIME: summer

HEIGHT/WIDTH: 2'–5' × 2' (60cm–1.5m × 60cm)

LIGHT: full sun–partial shade

ZONES: 3–9

Summer phlox

For a carnival of lively color and sweet scent, summer phlox is hard to beat. The widely available hybrids have completely superseded the wild species and come in a broad range of hues, from snowy white to pink to red to lavender and purple. Many have a contrasting center eye that adds extra sparkle. If you have the space, plant a mixture. Otherwise, you are sure to find at least one or two individual varieties that fit well into your garden's color scheme. One of the best is 'Bright Eyes', pastel pink with a crimson center. If you prefer a solid-color phlox, there are many to choose from. 'Starfire' is red to magenta with dark purple leaves; all-white 'David' is also an excellent choice.

Phlox blooms heavily for weeks on end, provided you have planted it in the same rich, moist soil it thrives on in the wild. Horticulturists have not managed to conquer the plant's one flaw, susceptibility to powdery mildew, which attacks toward the end of the season. A little extra room for air circulation may help—either plant individuals fairly well apart at the outset, or do some thinning after the plants are up and growing in the spring. Spraying with "antitranspirants" (ask at your local garden center) also seems to help. An easier recourse, though, is to plant resistant varieties, of which there are many new ones. Ask, or read catalog descriptions carefully.

Physostegia virginiana

Obedient plant

BLOOM TIME: mid–late summer

HEIGHT/WIDTH: 1'–3' × 8"–2' (30–90cm × 20–60cm)

LIGHT: full sun

ZONES: 3–9

Obedient plant

The curious common name of this wildflower refers to the alleged ability of individual flowers to stay in place when nudged. The plant is related to the snapdragon (the flowers are superficially similar), but, truth be told, it is no more cooperative. Nonetheless, children, especially, like to try tweaking the flowers this way and that.

The real excitement about this plant is its wonderful performance in hot, oppressive, humid summer weather. The stems continue to stand tall through it all, lined with handsome, unflagging dark green foliage and tirelessly producing a dependable supply of pretty flowers for weeks.

Obedient plant is related to mint, and has the same square stems—and the same tendency to grow rampantly in moist soil. If you grow it in average to dry soil, however, you need never see this side of its personality.

The flowers of the species are pink, but some wildflower nurseries offer other choices. Look for darker-hued 'Bouquet Rose' or white 'Summer Snow'. A relatively new selection, 'Variegata', sports cream-striped leaves, a nifty contrast to the pink blooms. Boltonia and wild species of aster have an overlapping bloom time and look lovely with obedient plant.

Polemonium reptans

Jacob's-ladder

BLOOM TIME: spring

HEIGHT/WIDTH: 1'–2' × 1'–2' (30–60cm × 30–60cm)

LIGHT: full sun–partial shade

ZONES: 4–8

Jacob's-ladder

You would never guess that a flower this ferny of foliage and delicate of flower was related to phlox. Yet it is, and it shares with that group sweet scent, soft bloom color, and a clump-forming growth habit. That is where the resemblance ends, however.

The small, dainty flowers are especially sweet: they are airy little China-blue bells accented with tiny white stamens. They appear in clusters at the tips of the plants, so that a patch in full bloom has a fairyland quality. Among the wildflowers that make enchanting companions are foamflower and Virginia bluebells.

It is the leaves that give the plant its common name. They are arranged along the rather brittle stems in pairs, growing smaller as they ascend. They reminded someone of the biblical story of Jacob's dream of ascending to heaven on the rungs of a ladder. Unlike some spring-blooming wildflowers, the leaves of this plant remain all season.

This particular species, native to the East Coast from New York south to Alabama, has a more creeping habit than the more commonly grown *P. caeruleum*, so it is a better choice for planting in sweeps or naturalizing. Grow it in rich, moist soil for best performance.

Polygonatum odoratum

Solomon's seal

BLOOM TIME: spring

HEIGHT/WIDTH: 1'–2' × 1'–2' (30–60cm × 30–60cm)

LIGHT: partial–full shade

ZONES: 4–8

'Variegatum' Solomon's seal

This elegant plant, grown mainly for its foliage, has a wonderful presence in the garden. Strong, graceful stems spread outward, bearing along their length oval-shaped, parallel-veined leaves. Dangling along the underside of the stem in spring is a jaunty row of diminutive, pale green to white, lightly perfumed, bell-shaped flowers. These become blue-black berries by late summer.

The beautiful 'Variegatum' has leaf edges and tips splashed with white markings, which looks fabulous among hostas. If you have the space and want an even bolder show, try Great Solomon's seal (a hybrid of *P. biflorum* or *P. commutatum*), whose arching stems can be 6 feet (1.8m) long.

Solomon's seal has been grown around the world for a long time. The source of the name seems lost to history, though there are several theories. If you examine the tuberous roots, you'll see round scars from the previous year's stalks—these are said to resemble Solomon's seal, or signet. (By the way, you'll be able to determine a plant's age by counting these scars.) Another explanation is that, used medicinally, the plant was useful for healing, or sealing, wounds. Yet another possibility is that the six-pointed flowers were taken to resemble the six points of the Star of David, which was once called "Solomon's seal."

Pontederia cordata

Pickerel rush

BLOOM TIME: late summer

HEIGHT/WIDTH: 2'–3' × 2'–3' (60–90cm × 60–90cm)

LIGHT: full sun

ZONES: 5–9

Pickerel rush

This native of marshes and ponds is an excellent choice for a water garden or boggy area. Unlike some other water-loving plants, it does not look weedy and it is not invasive. Instead, it forms handsome, well-mannered clumps. Pickerel rush is simple to grow, provided its requirement for ample water is met. If you pot it and place it by the edge of a garden pool, immerse it no more than 6 inches (15cm) deep. In other settings, don't let it dry out.

The glossy green leaves are broadly spear-shaped; in the latter part of the summer, they are joined by dense spikes of light blue to royal purple flowers. Aquatics nurseries also offer it in white and, more recently, pink. It will bloom more heavily if fertilized monthly during the growing season, and half-tablets of waterlily fertilizer are fine for this purpose.

Pickerel rush is a valuable addition to a water garden. Its late bloom time brings welcome color at a time when few other accent plants are blooming. The blue combines well with many waterlilies, especially yellow or red ones—the spikes are dense enough to provide significant contrast, and the plant's vertical habit makes the display more interesting. When the plant is not in bloom, the foliage is sufficiently healthy and an effective foil for the flat lily pads and strap-like leaves of many other pondside growers.

Ratibida pinnata

Prairie coneflower

BLOOM TIME: summer

HEIGHT/WIDTH: 2'–5' × 1'–2' (60cm–1.5m × 30–60cm)

LIGHT: full sun

ZONES: 4–8

Prairie coneflower

Tall and showy, the prairie, or gray-headed, coneflower is a fun flower for low-maintenance areas of your yard. It is not fussy about soil, tolerating everything from damp to dry situations—all it requires is plenty of sun. Because of its stature and casual profile, it would be ideal along a fence, toward the back of a wildflower border, or in a meadow planting. Warning: as with many prairie natives, the clumps of this plant form a ranging, fibrous root system, making later transplanting difficult and perhaps requiring stern control measures if it exceeds its allotted space.

The flowers look like little shuttlecocks, with 1- or 2-inch (2.5 or 5cm) bright yellow petals ("ray flowers") swooping back from the prominent center cone. The cone is gray-green to start, but darkens over the course of the summer. The plant pumps these out by the dozens for weeks on end. They are wonderful in flower arrangements, keeping for many days. They also dry well.

Romneya coulteri

Matilija poppy

BLOOM TIME: late spring–early summer

HEIGHT/WIDTH: 6'–8' × 3'–6' (1.8–2.4m × 1–1.8m)

LIGHT: full sun–partial shade

ZONES: 6–9

Matilija poppy

It's taller than you are, it has gray-green, divided leaves, and the huge crepe-paper flowers with the bright boss of golden stamens are unmistakably poppies. What can it be? This exuberant relative of the more familiar Oriental poppies is a California native—though it can be grown in other areas with mild climates. All it requires is sun and soil that drains well (in nature, it is found in dry canyons and washes below four thousand feet [1,200m]). The magnificent flowers are pleasantly fragrant and are followed by those familiar poppy seed capsules.

Matilija poppy is so big and billowing that it is best treated as if it were a shrub. Some gardeners use it as a foundation plant with shorter drought-tolerant plants in front of it. It also makes a good curb-strip plant because it is so tough and so dramatic. Just plant it where you want it to stay, because it is not easily moved. A mature plant has an extensive, fleshy root system that resents being disturbed. It does tend to sucker, and you can dig these up while they are still small and plant them elsewhere or give them away to admiring friends.

Rudbeckia hirta

Black-eyed Susan

BLOOM TIME: summer

HEIGHT/WIDTH: 18"–3' × 2'–3' (45–90cm × 60–90cm)

LIGHT: full sun

ZONES: 4–9

Black-eyed Susan

One of the biggest success stories in wildflowers-gone-to-gardens is the sturdy black-eyed Susan. It pumps out large numbers of especially big, bold flowers, which helps account for its popularity, but also brings with it a natural toughness. Not even the most neglectful gardener can say this plant is difficult to grow. Just give it full sun and ordinary soil. A drought-tolerant plant, it will survive on minimal water. Its only weakness is occasional powdery mildew on the leaves, best avoided by giving it ample elbow room.

There are a number of similar-looking species; *Rudbeckia hirta* is valued because it is reliably perennial, although it will also self-sow. The petals ("ray flowers") are cheerful orange-yellow, and the center cone is chocolaty brown, except when it is dusted with golden pollen. There are many worthy cultivated varieties and relatives.

All rudbeckias bloom over a long period in the garden and retain their color well. They also hold up in bouquets, fresh or dried, and don't readily drop their petals. Picking the hairy, tough stems can be a bit of a struggle, forcing you to resort to a sharp knife or scissors. The stems also remain straight in a vase or outdoors over the winter months. This is because they are lined with fine grooves—as students of architecture will tell you, a fluted column is stronger than a smooth one.

Sanguinaria canadensis

Bloodroot

BLOOM TIME: spring

HEIGHT/WIDTH: 6"–14" × 6"–8" (15–36cm × 15–20cm)

LIGHT: partial–full shade

ZONES: 3–8

'Multiplex' bloodroot

Bloodroot is a familiar sight in wooded areas of the Northeast in early spring, where it thrives in rich, moist, acidic soil. The deeply lobed but heart-shaped leaves are very distinctive, and the creamy white blossoms are lovely. Rock gardeners and connoisseurs of perennials often grow the gorgeous, double-flowered variety 'Multiplex'.

Alas, this pristine beauty has a short moment of glory—in ideal conditions under the shade of high trees, you can expect the blooms to last for only a week or so. They open fully during the day, and fold upward each evening like a closing umbrella; be forewarned that the petals are fragile, and will shatter when disturbed. Make the most of blood-

root's show, then, by planting it in an area where no other flowers will compete for attention (until, of course, the blooms are gone), such as among ferns or later-blooming perennial groundcovers such as European or American ginger. Bloodroot's uniquely shaped leaves will linger on for the rest of the season if your soil is not too dry.

By the way, the common name refers to the plant's juicy, orange-red sap, which bleeds from a clipped stem or nicked root and colors skin and fabric easily. It was once used medicinally but is now considered dangerous, due to the presence of a toxic alkaloid.

Sarracenia spp.

Pitcher plant

BLOOM TIME: spring

HEIGHT/WIDTH: 6"–3' × 4"–1' (15–90cm × 10–30cm)

LIGHT: full sun

ZONES: Most are hardy in zones 7–10

Pitcher plant

Yes, they eat bugs, but aren't they gorgeous? Pitcher plants lure bees, flies, and other insects with nectar and scent glands located on the treacherous interior of their lovely, fluted leaf structures; the unsuspecting victims follow deeper and deeper into the plant until they slip into a brew of water and enzymes that consumes them. The theory is that the resulting rich liquid produced nourishes the plants, which grow naturally in an otherwise rather nutrient-poor setting (soggy, acidic wetlands).

In recent years, gardeners have been flocking to pitcher plants because they are beautiful. The leaves come in many colors and patterns, from the green and maroon fili-gree of *S. leucophylla* to the lavender-and-purple veined *S. purpurea* and *S. rubra*. The odd-looking flowers, which appear atop their own slender stalk, may be anything from maroon to acid yellow—they don't last long, however, so the leaves remain the main attraction.

There is no mystery to growing a patch of pitcher plants. If your property lacks an acidic bog, you can mimic one easily enough by filling a shallow container with damp peat moss lightened with some sand for the sake of drainage. Keep the medium wet at all times. If you observe mineral salts building up on the surface, flush out the pot well so the delicate plants aren't adversely affected.

Sedum ternatum

Stonecrop

BLOOM TIME: spring

HEIGHT/WIDTH: 3"–8" × 8"–15" (7–20cm × 20–38cm)

LIGHT: partial shade

ZONES: 4–7

Stonecrop

There are plenty of fancier and showier sedums, to be sure, but the classic species has its virtues. For one, it's simple to grow, requiring only well-drained soil. It establishes itself quickly and forms handsome, spreading mats that require barely any attention except maybe a little tidying early each spring.

It has succulent foliage, like other sedums; its leaves are an attractive shade of blue-green. Stonecrop's sprawling growth habit makes it ideal for banks or slopes in a wild part of the garden, or trailing over rocks or a stone wall in a conventional rock garden setting. Its relatively shallow root system and easygoing nature mean you can tuck other plants in and around it—or let it form a carpet at the base of shrubs.

Each spring, you get the bonus of several weeks of flowers. These are little white stars, less than an inch (2.5cm) across but borne in sprays for greater impact.

Shortia galacifolia

Oconee bells

BLOOM TIME: late spring–early summer

HEIGHT/WIDTH: 6"–8" × 6"–8" (15–20cm × 15–20cm)

LIGHT: partial–full shade

ZONES: 5–8

Oconee bells

When you see this wildflower in bloom, you really do expect to see tiny fairies flitting nearby. The 1-inch (2.5cm) white (sometimes pinkish) bells—actually rather large for a plant this diminutive—have fringed petal edges and sherbet-yellow centers. These bloom for a week or two each spring, and are accompanied by rosettes of durable, glossy green, heart-shaped leaves. There is only one flower per plant, so planting in groups or as a groundcover is wise. It loses impact when you mix it with a lot of other wildflowers or overbearing ferns, though you could slip a few plants into a rock garden here and there. It is also nice in a rhododendron or azalea glade, plants it is seen with in the wild.

This charmer hails from the wildflower-rich Appalachian mountains, but it is winter-hardy as far north as southern New England. As the weather gets colder, the handsome leaves take on a reddish-bronze hue. To succeed with oconee bells, you should simulate the conditions it enjoys in its natural home: acidic, moist, humusy soil and partial shade is ideal. It will adapt to more sun, if you mulch it, and heavier soils, provided you dig in some peat moss or compost prior to planting. It tends to be slow to get established, but long-lived.

Silene virginica

Fire pink

BLOOM TIME: spring

HEIGHT/WIDTH: 1'–2' × 1' (30–60cm × 30cm)

LIGHT: partial shade–full sun

ZONES: 3–8

Fire pink

Here is a wildflower that, when brought into a garden setting, completely outshines its performance in nature. Its native habitat is dry, rocky slopes that receive some shade, conditions difficult to duplicate in cultivation. But plant it in full sun in your garden and you will find that the stems don't flop over nearly as much as they do in the wild. It will do fine in average (not rich) soil. Mulch it, water it regularly, and you will be astounded at its full, bushy profile, and the way the bright flowers literally cover the plant.

You'll welcome the bountiful flowering because the blooms are so terrific. Small tubes flare open to display long scarlet petals. These are slightly notched at their tips, giving away their relationship to carnations and dianthus, otherwise known as "pinks," hence the common name. The plant stays in bloom for several weeks. Try it in the company of white flowers, such as white phlox, dame's rocket, or daisies. In the wild, it consorts with blue phlox and violet wood sorrel, which should also work in the garden. No matter what companions you choose, allow your fire pink some room, as it doesn't enjoy being crowded.

Sisyrinchium angustifolium

Blue-eyed grass

BLOOM TIME: spring

HEIGHT/WIDTH: 6"–18" × 4"–6" (15–45cm × 10–15cm)

LIGHT: full sun

ZONES: 4–9

Blue-eyed grass

Few grasses or grasslike plants have flowers worth mentioning, at least from the point of view of a gardener. This perky little plant is the exception. Its star-shaped flowers are sky blue to periwinkle, centered with a small, cheerful splash of yellow. These appear in clusters rather than one to a stem, adding to their impact. A South American relative, *S. striatum*, has cream-colored flowers.

Nonetheless, you will have to site the plant with care if you want to enjoy the flowers, as they are small, only ½-inch (1.5cm) across. Tuck a few specimens into a rock garden, a mixed container planting, or the front of a flower border.

Despite its name, blue-eyed grass is actually in the iris family, which accounts for its preference for shallow growing conditions and soil that is on the damp side. The soil should also be of average quality (rich soil causes excessive foliage at the expense of flowering). Be sure your plants receive adequate light and elbow room so they don't have to compete for resources. Then, you'll find that your garden-grown plants flower much more lustily than their counterparts in the wild.

Smilacina racemosa

False Solomon's seal

BLOOM TIME: spring

HEIGHT/WIDTH: 1'–3' × 1' (30–90cm × 30cm)

LIGHT: partial shade

ZONES: 3–7

False Solomon's seal

Because this is a relatively tall, erect woodland plant, you may find it better suited to being placed among larger plants than some of the other, lower-growing groundcovering wildflowers. Try false Solomon's seal among rhododendrons and azaleas or big-leaved hostas (it prefers the same moist, acidic soil they do), or skirting the base of a shade tree. It offers long, graceful stems lined with glossy, pleated leaves.

It is known as "false" because it is similar to Solomon's seal (another genus entirely, *Polygonatum*) when out of bloom, though often not as large. Also, the flowers are completely different; they are cream-colored, starry, and borne in clusters at the stem tips; later, they become red, not blue, berries. A drift of false Solomon's seal in bloom is an arresting sight—plus, you will detect the flowers' pleasing fragrance.

Solidago spp.

Goldenrod

BLOOM TIME: midsummer to autumn

HEIGHT/WIDTH: varies

LIGHT: full sun

ZONES: 3–9

'Fireworks' goldenrod

Goldenrod is a real Cinderella story. Long scorned or overlooked as a weed, or avoided because it was falsely thought to cause hay fever (the real culprit is the less showy ragweed, which blooms at the same time), it is now enjoying praise and popularity. And no wonder. In full bloom, it is a glorious sight, and the bright color complements many other late-season bloomers. You'll love goldenrod with the yellow-centered New England asters—both the species and the bigger-bloomed cultivated varieties.

There are now some terrific garden hybrids. The best ones are well behaved enough to stay in bounds in your perennial borders, and feature plush plumes composed of tiny golden flowers. Like their wild cousins, these improved goldenrods are eager to bloom and easy to care for. The aptly named *S. rugosa* 'Fireworks' is a compact, dome-shaped, clump-forming plant (3 to 4 feet [90–120cm] tall) that cascades with bright yellow color. *S. sphacelata* 'Golden Fleece' is a dwarf selection (1½ to 2 feet [45–60cm] tall) that carries its cheery sprays in a tidy, pyramidal fashion. *S. virgaurea* 'Crown of Rays' (2 feet [60cm] tall) has such full, lush plumes that it looks like a golden waterfall.

All of these do fine in poor to average soil—in fact, soil that is too rich will cause them to grow more rampantly than you might wish.

Stokesia laevis

Stokes' aster

BLOOM TIME: summer

HEIGHT/WIDTH: 1'–2' × 1'–2' (30–60cm × 30–60cm)

LIGHT: full sun

ZONES: 5–9

'Cyanea' Stokes' aster

If you like blue flowers and want something that's durable and low-maintenance, consider the lovely Stokes' aster. Its long-lasting blooms are wonderfully intricate and delicate-looking. The flower heads are large, about 4 inches (10cm) across, and feature two rows of numerous petals; the outer ones spray outward in a loose, open fashion, while the shorter, inner ones hug close to the center. The effect is a bit like a Chinese aster, or maybe a bachelor's button. In any event, they're produced one-to-a-stalk, which is a plus for bouquet lovers (also, they tend to have a long vase life). They are usually lavender-blue, but there are also many fine cultivars. 'Alba', of course, has white flowers. 'Klaus Jelitto' has powder-blue blooms. Those of 'Wyoming' are especially dark blue.

The plant is a mound-former, covered in smooth, spear-shaped leaves that make a nice contrast to the interesting flowers. Stokes' aster is wonderfully adaptable and fairly cold-hardy, despite the fact that its natural habitat, the coastal plain of the southeastern United States, is rather restricted. It is happiest in soil that drains well and is neither too fertile nor too poor (it can even be grown at the seashore). Don't overwater it or plant it in a spot that gets waterlogged in the winter months.

Stylophorum diphyllum

Celandine poppy

BLOOM TIME: late spring–summer

HEIGHT/WIDTH: 12"–18" × 10"–15" (30–45cm × 25–38cm)

LIGHT: full sun–partial shade

ZONES: 4–8

Celandine poppy

There's no trick to growing this pretty, long-flowering poppy. It grows well in almost any spot, provided it gets the moisture it needs either from the soil or from the hose. Over the years, it will multiply, but it is not an aggressive plant like lesser celandine (*Ranunculus ficaria*).

The flowers are yellow and glossy, so even though they are small, about 2 inches (5cm) across, they capture your attention. They make a nice stand under the shelter of deciduous trees, mixing well with other spring-blooming wildflowers. But you might also tuck a few individual plants into your sunny flower garden, where their simple, cheery nature and bright color will be welcome. The fuzzy little seedpods (which may be on the plant at the same time as new flowers are opening—a charming sight) are characteristic of poppies. If you leave them be and have no chipmunks in your neighborhood to make off with the seeds, these poppy plants will self-sow.

The much-lobed foliage seems large for the flowers and is an attractive shade of blue-green that intermixes well with other plants. It looks particularly fine among ferns.

Thalictrum aquilegifolium

Meadow rue

BLOOM TIME: spring

HEIGHT/WIDTH: 2'–3' × 1' (60–90cm × 30cm)

LIGHT: full sun–partial shade

ZONES: 5–9

Meadow rue

Each spring, tiny lavender "beads" sway atop slender stalks, opening to enchanting little powder-puff blooms. The cultivar 'Album' has the same buds but — surprise — opens white. There is also a deeper purple one called 'Purple Cloud'.

Shorter than other meadow rues, this species does not require staking, but it is still tall enough to bring a little height to the middle or back of a flower bed. The *aquilegifolium* part of the name refers to the fact that the leaves are similar to those of columbine, that is, dainty and lacy. These are bluish green and clothe the stems at loose intervals, stopping short of the airy flower heads. Thanks to the foliage, the plant maintains a welcome graceful presence in the garden even after the flowers have come and gone.

The key to a sterling performance from meadow rue is moist soil, like that of its native habitat. A light mulch and some afternoon shade are a good idea in especially hot summers.

Thermopsis caroliniana

Carolina lupine, Carolina bush pea

BLOOM TIME: spring

HEIGHT/WIDTH: 3'–5' × 2'–3' (1–1.5m × 60–90cm)

LIGHT: full sun

ZONES: 5–8

Carolina lupine

A tallish, erect plant with striking flowers, Carolina lupine deserves to be more widely grown. It is well behaved enough to join a formal perennial border (imagine it with China blue campanulas) and easygoing enough to chime in with other bold-flowered plants in a more casual scheme (try it with baptisia or penstemon). Its needs are easily met: full sun, rich soil, supplementary water and/or mulch during dry spells.

It begins its season with bushy, dark green, cloverlike foliage and is soon joined by the dense flowering stalks, which rise above the leaves. The large sunny yellow flowers, which last for weeks and weeks, look a great deal like lupine blooms. Later, they fade to flattened brown seedpods.

A couple of minor caveats: young plants are slow to bloom, spending their first season or two on root development instead—so you have to be patient. Also, Carolina lupine forms a deep taproot, so site it where you want it to stay, as later transplanting may not be possible.

Tiarella cordifolia

Foamflower

BLOOM TIME: spring

HEIGHT/WIDTH: 6"–12" × 6"–12" (15–30cm × 15–30cm)

LIGHT: shade

ZONES: 3–8

Foamflower

No doubt this irresistible woodland wildflower gets its common name from the way it literally foams with airy white blossoms for many weeks each spring—a sight best enjoyed when it is growing in large groups. You can reproduce this show easily in your own shady garden, provided you have humus-rich soil (naturally found under deciduous trees).

Foamflower's blooms aren't actually pure white. Tiny golden stamens shoot outward amid the white petals, giving individual blooms a starry look and the entire spike a full yet exuberant appearance. The leaves are equally handsome, and carry on well after the flowers are gone, as long as you remember to water the plants during the heat of summer. They are heart-shaped, somewhat furry, and in the variety *T. cordifolia* var. *collina* (also known as *T. wherryi*) feature accenting red veins. Foamflower leaves gain an attractive bronze hue as cold weather arrives.

So agreeable and good-looking is foamflower that native-plant nurseries have been answering the call for variations. Among the alternatives you may find are clump-forming 'Dunvegan', with pink-tinted flowers and sage-green leaves, and delicate-looking but eager-growing 'Slickrock', with smaller, deeply lobed forest green leaves and light pink blooms.

Tradescantia virginiana

Spiderwort

BLOOM TIME: summer

HEIGHT/WIDTH: 1'–2' × 3' (30–60cm × 90cm)

LIGHT: full sun–partial shade

ZONES: 5–8

'Concord Grape' spiderwort

Clumps of grassy leaves that may remind you of daylily foliage will enthusiastically cover a bank, line a pathway, or serve as a foundation planting, with the added bonus of a constant supply of flowers. Spiderwort leaves can be a foot or more long and interweave and overlap, generally to the exclusion of weeds. The distinctive, three-petaled flowers look a bit like little tricorner Colonial hats, are centered with a small boss of yellow-tipped stamens, and are carried in umbels. Between 1 and 2 inches (2.5–5cm) across, they are usually blue. Deadheading is not necessary—the petals fade and drop unobtrusively each evening to be replaced by others coming into bloom the next morning. If the show begins to dissipate or the foliage starts to sprawl, simply cut back the entire plant hard; by autumn, you should get a repeat performance.

The native spiderwort is a tough plant, prospering in sun or part shade; some shade makes the color of the leaves and flowers darker. It tolerates all sorts of soil and moisture conditions. In damp spots, it will grow rampantly. It also self-sows, so plan for its eager growth by putting it in a spot where you want a lot of ground covered.

Trillium grandiflorum

Large-flowered trillium

BLOOM TIME: spring

HEIGHT/WIDTH: 12"–18" × 8"–12" (30–45cm × 20–30cm)

LIGHT: partial–full shade

ZONES: 3–9

Large-flowered trillium

Alas, this is one wildflower we may have to live without—in our gardens. It is undeniably beautiful, and familiar to anyone who has taken a walk in shady, moist woods in early spring. There, it looks both sturdy and plentiful, displaying its broad white flowers with grace as it carpets large areas.

But trilliums are endangered plants in many areas. It's not the depredations of an occasional admiring hiker that threaten the wild populations (though the plant makes a poor cut flower and is very unlikely to survive transplanting back home), it's the pillaging done by wildflower poachers.

Professional horticulturists are desperately seeking a fast, easy way to propagate them. Unfortunately, offsets naturally produced by the rhizomes are few and slow to get established. Tissue culture (raising clones in laboratory test tubes) does generate more little trilliums but there is about a five-year wait for blooming-size plants. Trillium can also be grown from freshly harvested seed, but blooms may be up to nine years away! So, needless to say, an inexpensive trillium plant from a local or mail-order nursery should be viewed with great suspicion. Your best bet, if you simply must have trillium, is to check the plant sales of botanical gardens—and pay the high price willingly. Otherwise, if demand for trillium continues unabated, we won't have them in the woods *or* our gardens.

Uvularia sessilifolia

Wild oats, sessile bellwort

BLOOM TIME: spring

HEIGHT/WIDTH: 1' × 1' (30cm × 30cm)

LIGHT: partial shade

ZONES: 3–8

Wild oats

Dry shade? No problem. Here's a sweet little groundcover that you can plant, give a little mulch, let spread, and leave alone. It may remind you somewhat of Solomon's seal, thanks to its arching stems lined with oval, tapering leaves, but this is a smaller plant, generally with fewer leaves to a stem. Wild oats has the curious habit of leaning in one direction, something that becomes more noticeable and actually quite charming when you grow it en masse.

The dainty, 1-inch (2.5cm), bell-shaped flowers, which appear at the ends of the stems, are soft yellow.

Unfortunately, they hang downward, so they're not very noticeable, though they do last for several weeks. In and out of bloom, wild oats looks good in the company of smaller, airy ferns and wildflowers of similar stature, such as Virginia bluebells.

Related species are larger of stem and flower. Strawbells, *U. perfoliata*, reaches 2 feet (60cm). Merrybells, *U. grandiflora*, is taller, grows up to 30 inches (76cm), and also has a more erect growth habit.

Verbascum spp.

Mullein

BLOOM TIME: summer

HEIGHT/WIDTH: 4'–8' × 3' (1.2–2.4m × 90cm)

LIGHT: full sun

ZONES: 5–9

Mullein

If you've been dismissing this stately plant as a roadside weed, you're missing out. Granted, it grows as easily as weed (all it wants is well-drained or dry soil), but don't let that blind you to its virtues. Mullein's profile is husky enough to make an important contribution to a cottage garden scheme. And it looks wonderful in the company of roses, particularly the old-fashioned ones. Gardeners in the Southwest and West sometimes group three or so plants center stage or as a foil to boulders or a wall; mulleins certainly have the presence to succeed in such settings.

Most are biennials, so all you see their first summer is a large, felted, gray-leaved rosette hugging the ground. Their second summer, though, is worth waiting for. Then, substantial spires rise up and display their blooms for many, many weeks. Some species have branched spires for a candelabra effect, desirable if you want maximum impact.

A tour of the flower colors may further persuade you. A number of mulleins (among them *V. bombyciferum*, *V. olympicum*, and *V. thapsus*) are a pleasant primrose yellow. Some are white-flowered, a soft duet with the silvery foliage (*V. chaixii* 'Album', *V.* × *hybridum* 'Mont Blanc'). The variable *V. phoeniceum* ranges from red to pink to white, but is usually seen lavender. The 'Southern Charm' hybrids are pastels from apricot to soft pink to light purple.

Vernonia novaboracensis

Ironweed

BLOOM TIME: late summer

HEIGHT/WIDTH: 5'–8' × 2'–4' (1.5–2.4m × 60cm–120cm)

LIGHT: full sun

ZONES: 5–7

Ironweed

Have you read the Pulitzer prize–winning novel by William Kennedy named after this plant? He did his homework: the introduction, adapted from the Audubon Society's wild-flower guide, notes that ironweed owes its name to the toughness of its stem. Kennedy's hero, Frank Phelan, has great tenacity in the face of all sorts of misfortunes.

In addition to the strong, erect stem that sees this tow-ering wildflower through wind and weather, ironweed has another laudable asset. The electric purple flowers, borne in clusters, are probably the most vivid shade of purple you can expect to see at that time of year (did Kennedy also want to point out Phelan's intensity?).

Ironweed is not at all particular about soil. It will do fine in lean soil, and be a bit bigger and lusher in more fer-tile spots. Set some of the newer, abundant-flowering gold-enrods at its base for a great shout of late-season color. Or line it up along a garage wall or back fence with tall sun-flowers. It is not an especially good self-sower.

Veronicastrum virginicum

Culver's root

BLOOM TIME: summer

HEIGHT/WIDTH: 4'–7' × 1'–3' (1.2–2m × 30–90cm)

LIGHT: full sun

ZONES: 3–9

Culver's root

Where your sunny garden can use the height, this slender, graceful plant will be a wonderful addition. As you might guess from the name, it is closely related to the familiar garden perennial veronica (in fact, it was formerly classified as one). The difference, of course, is the size, and the habit as well; veronica is often a mound, wider than tall, while this plant is taller and much more narrow.

Otherwise, the blooms are quite similar to those of Veronica—pretty, tapering spires composed of tiny flowers. The species is either white or a soft blue; the blue hue is especially apparent when you view a large planting from a distance.

Horticulturists have made an effort to select for consistent color, and, if you wish, you can choose pristine 'Album' (also known as var. album) or pale pink 'Roseum' (also known as var. rosea). Whatever the color, the spires hold up well in a vase and also dry well for arrangements.

Like so many other native wildflowers, Culver's root thrives in fertile soil that drains well; a mulch is advisable where summers are long and hot. You would do well to plant it in groupings so the flowers stand out well. Then give it some attractive, taller companions that like similar conditions, such as bee balm or Joe-Pye weed.

Viola pedata

Bird-foot violet

BLOOM TIME: spring and autumn

HEIGHT/WIDTH: 4"–10" × 4"–6" (10–25cm × 10–15cm)

LIGHT: full sun–partial shade

ZONES: 4–9

Bird-foot violet

All the wild violets are sweet, delicate things, but the bird-foot may be the loveliest. Its name comes from its unique leaves, which, rather than the usual heart shape, are finely divided (between nine and fifteen points) to look a bit like a many-toed small bird's foot.

The flowers of this violet are also bigger than some of its near relatives, up to an inch and a half (4cm)across. And unlike the ubiquitous Johnny-jump-ups, they're violet, though sometimes the three lower petals are a contrasting lighter hue. Tiny stamens are golden to orange. Bird-foot violet flowers have a soft, romantic fragrance. They bloom in the spring, and often again in the autumn, especially if you remember to cut back the plants to within a few inches of the ground several weeks after flowering.

To thrive in a garden setting, bird-foot violet must have sharply drained soil. It languishes in rich soil, and develops crown rot if its spot is too damp. So perhaps the best place for it is a pathside, slope, or bank that is sandy or gravelly—a site where few other plants will grow anyway. If you'd like to include it in the garden proper, you can line its planting hole with a handful of sand or grit. Its graceful, rather lacy character is pretty among spring-flowering bulbs.

PLANT HARDINESS ZONES

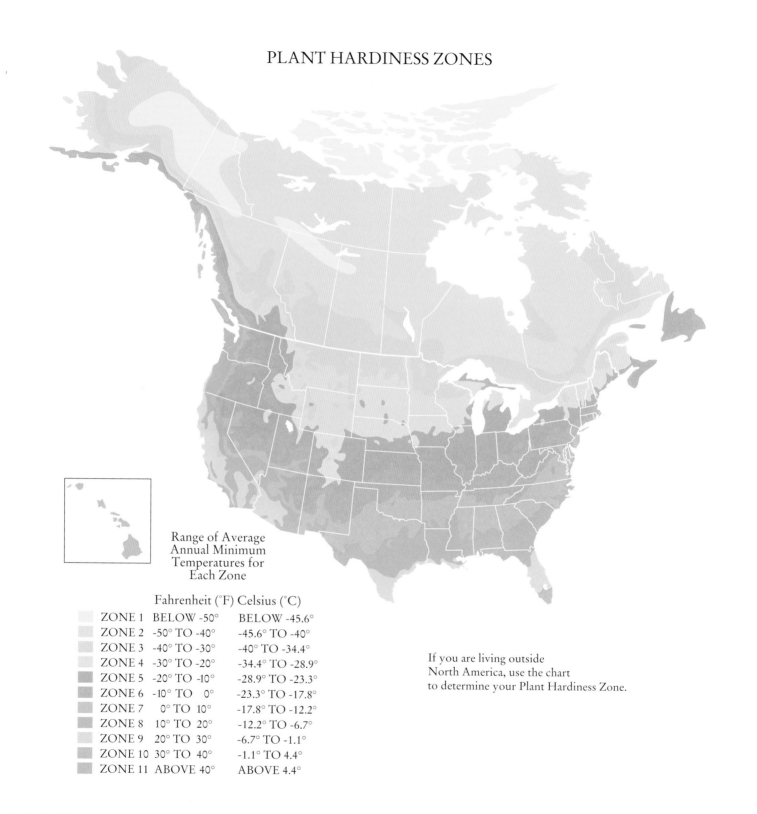

Range of Average
Annual Minimum
Temperatures for
Each Zone

	Fahrenheit (°F)	Celsius (°C)
ZONE 1	BELOW -50°	BELOW -45.6°
ZONE 2	-50° TO -40°	-45.6° TO -40°
ZONE 3	-40° TO -30°	-40° TO -34.4°
ZONE 4	-30° TO -20°	-34.4° TO -28.9°
ZONE 5	-20° TO -10°	-28.9° TO -23.3°
ZONE 6	-10° TO 0°	-23.3° TO -17.8°
ZONE 7	0° TO 10°	-17.8° TO -12.2°
ZONE 8	10° TO 20°	-12.2° TO -6.7°
ZONE 9	20° TO 30°	-6.7° TO -1.1°
ZONE 10	30° TO 40°	-1.1° TO 4.4°
ZONE 11	ABOVE 40°	ABOVE 4.4°

If you are living outside
North America, use the chart
to determine your Plant Hardiness Zone.

Sources

Although certain wildflowers plants can be found in the offerings of general nursery catalogs, the following nurseries either specialize in them or have particularly broad selections. Please remember to include the fee for the catalog; it covers the cost of printing and mailing.

Donaroma's Nursery
P.O. Box 2189
Edgartown, MA 02539
Free catalog

Heronswood Nursery
7530 N.E. 288th St.
Kingston, WA 98346
Catalog $5

J.L. Hudson, Seedsman
Star Route 2, Box 337
La Honda, CA 94020
Catalog $2

Moon Mountain Wildflowers
P.O. Box 725
Carpinteria, CA 93014
Catalog $3

Native Gardens
5737 Fisher Lane
Greenback, TN 37742
Catalog $2

Niche Gardens
1111 Dawson Rd.
Chapel Hill, NC 27516
Catalog $3

Plants of the Southwest
Route 6, Box 11A
Santa Fe, NM 87501
Catalog $3.50

Prairie Nursery
P.O. Box 306
Westfield, WI 53964
Free catalog

Seeds Trust/High Altitude
Gardens
P.O. Box 1048
Hailey, ID 83333
Free catalog

Shooting Star Nursery
444 Bates Road
Frankfort, KY 40601
Catalog $2

Sunlight Gardens
174 Golden Lane
Andersonville, TN 37705
Catalog $3

Vermont Wildflower Farm
P.O. Box 5
Charlotte, VT 05445
Free catalog

We-Du Nurseries
Route 5, Box 724
Marion, NC 28752
Catalog $2

Wildseed Farms
425 Wildflower Hills
Fredericksburg, TX 78624
Catalog $2

Australian Sources

Country Farm Perennials
RSD Laings Road
Nayook VIC 3821

Cox's Nursery
RMB 216 Oaks Road
Thrilmere NSW 2572

Honeysuckle Cottage Nursery
Lot 35 Bowen Mountain Road
Bowen Mountain via Grosevale
NSW 2753

Swan Bros Pty Ltd
490 Galston Road
Dural NSW 2158

Canadian Sources

Corn Hill Nursery Ltd.
RR 5
Petitcodiac NB EOA 2HO

Ferncliff Gardens
SS 1
Mission, British Columbia
V2V 5V6

McFayden Seed Co. Ltd.
Box 1800
Brandon, Manitoba
R7A 6N4

Stirling Perennials
RR 1
Morpeth, Ontario
N0P 1X0

Organizations

Most states and provinces have a
native plant society, which can be
a great resource for beginning
wildflower gardeners; ask a local
landscaper, inquire at a good local
nursery or botanic garden, or try
the nearest cooperative extension
office. These groups meet
regularly, sharing information,
resources, and ideas, and
often have newsletters, plant
sales/swaps, and symposia.

Two of the biggest are well worth
contacting or visiting for a wealth
of information:

National Wildflower Research
Center
4801 LaCrosse Ave.
Austin, TX 78739
512-292-4200
www.wildflower.org

New England Wild Flower
Society
Hemenway Road
Framingham, MA 01701
(508) 877-7630
www.newfs.org/[tilde]newfs/

Further Reading

Basic Seed Saving
Bill McDorman
Pahsimeroi Press, 1994

Born in the Spring
June Carver Roberts
Ohio University Press, 1977

*A Garden of Wildflowers: 101 Native
Species and How to Grow Them*
Henry W. Art
Storey Communications, 1986

Growing and Propagating Wildflowers
Harry R. Phillips
University of North Carolina
Press, 1985

*Growing Wildflowers: A Gardener's
Guide*
Marie Sperka
Charles Scribner's Sons, 1984

A Guide to Enjoying Wildflowers
Donald and Lillian Stokes
Little-Brown, 1985

Newcomb's Wildflower Guide
Lawrence Newcomb; illustrated
by Gordon Morrison
Little-Brown, 1997

The Prairie Garden
J. Robert Smith, Beatrice S. Smith
University of Wisconsin Press,
1987

*The Wildflower Meadow Book:
A Gardener's Guide*
Laura C. Martin
Globe Pequot Press, 1986

*A Gardener's Encyclopedia
of Wildflowers*
C. Colston Burrell
Rodale Press, 1997

*Wildflowers in Your Garden:
A Gardener's Guide*
Viki Ferreniea
Random House, 1993